# The Difference I s t h e S o n

**Dr. Daniel
SHAYESTEH**
Author

*The Difference is The Son*

Copyright © 2004 by Daniel Shayesteh

Requests for information should be addressed to the author:

PO Box 1885, Castle Hill NSW 1765, Australia

ISBN: O-9756017-1-7

Cover Design: Janet Shayesteh

Published by Daniel Shayesteh

# Acknowledgments

It is an honour for me to acknowledge that without the inspiring encouragement, care, help and contributions provided by so many people, the completion of this book would not have been possible. English is my second language. Therefore, I had difficulty in expressing some of my personal and cultural feelings into words that could sufficiently carry the same or similar meaning in English. For this reason, I owe a debt of gratitude to my children, and to those who devoted their time tirelessly to reading my manuscript, assisting me to appropriately convey the message of this book.

My endless appreciation also goes to my wife and children. They have endured a life of simplicity with limited opportunities for many years. They did not push me to get secular full-time employment that would have hindered me from carrying out my researching and writing. Their loving attitude towards the world's nations has now allowed me to share my life experiences with many.

I humbly consider myself a student, gleaning priceless words, knowledge and wisdom from those that have studied and evaluated various beliefs and human history. Those who have gone before me have encouraged people to further investigation and the gaining of wisdom that will influence future decisions. My prayer is that this book may achieve the same outcome for those who desire to investigate and discover the truth.

# Contents

# Forward

We all know the tensions and often mistrust that exists between the 'East' and the 'West' in our world today. These divisions have deep historical roots and the scale of the differences often overwhelms us when we try and imagine a pathway to Peace.

"The Difference is the Son" is a significant book for all people who share a love of God's kingdom and God's blueprint for Peace through Jesus Christ. This book represents the thinking and feelings of a man who has seen and experienced the diverse cultural, religious and political landscapes of both the middle-eastern world and the west. As a result the book provides us with a valuable perspective from one who is qualified to speak by the very nature of his personal journey.

In order to fully appreciate what Daniel has written here, it is helpful for the reader to know something about Daniel's journey.

Daniel was born in Northern Iran near the beautiful shores and hinterlands of the Caspian Sea. He grew up in a nominal Islamic farming family near a small city. His sharp intellect was identified early on and he was encouraged to be a servant of Islam. By the age of 9 he was able to recite the Qur'an in Arabic.

During his teenage years he became interested in Islamic aesthetic philosophy (Erfaan, similar to

Sufism). During this time Daniel grew in his love of poetry and music.

He went off to university even though his family could only provide him with limited financial support. Daniel studied commerce and became a student communist during his first year of university. However, after reading various books on philosophy, he became convinced that there was one God for this universe. He therefore returned to Islam, but this time it was fundamentalist Islam.

Daniel was deeply involved in the Iranian Fundamentalist Revolution (1979) as a leading Muslim political leader and teacher of Islam in his homeland. Many years later he was saved wonderfully by Christ, when he escaped to Turkey after falling out of favor with Khomeini's political group.

Following is some of Daniel's story in his own words.

"Mary and I were born into nominal Muslim families in a small city in Iran. We became fully involved in the fundamentalist Islamic movement shortly after the Islamic Revolution. Our common interest in the movement drew us together and we were married. This involvement caused me to advance in the politically oriented religion "Islam", and with the recognition and support of people in our city I announced my candidacy for the Islamic Parliament.

The bitter rivalry of Islamic politics, which often leads to people being killed for their beliefs, meant I was a threat to Khomeini's political group who wanted to govern at any cost. I was kidnapped by Khomeini's Revolutionary Military and placed in a death cell to await a death sentence. God in his love and graciousness had other plans for my life and unexpectedly I was temporarily released, but I was not allowed to work in my city, and neither was I allowed to leave my city to seek work in other areas. Finally, after two attempts, I escaped into Turkey - homeless and without family or friends. My loneliness was overwhelming at the time and I feared for my family's safety because of my escape.

A year later in Turkey, through a business deal that went wrong, I came into contact with a Christian group who encouraged and supported me during this time.

One day I came to believe that the world and everything in it, including myself, was unjust. I started to complain to God (which god?), saying "Aren't you the almighty god? Should I suffer all my life? What is this life for? How can I get out of this life?"

That night I heard Jesus' voice in a dream, and the following Sunday I heard the preacher saying the exact words Jesus said to me in the dream: "Come out of your old house and build a new house on the rock of Jesus" (based on Luke 6:48f). At the time, I didn't know that there is only one Almighty Name by which man can be saved.

Yes, only one Name, Jesus.

The preacher's invitation created a desire in my heart to ask for a book (New Testament), which would give me knowledge of Him through His words. And I read, "for just as through the disobedience of the one man the many were made sinners, so also through the obedience of the one man the many will be made righteous" (Romans 5:19). Logically and philosophically, I realized that all the fullness of the Deity lives in the second man (Jesus) (Col. 2:9-10) and He is able to save sinners. This also, unlike other religions' philosophy, revealed to me a new and genuine philosophy that, "God is personal and I can have an eternal relationship with Him".

Therefore, I believed in Him as my Creator, Saviour and Deliverer.

Months later Mary and the children joined me in Turkey. My conversion came as a shock to my wife. "How can a person change his or her religion?" were her words, yet she recognized a change in me. Some time later Jesus appeared to Mary in a dream, and through God's goodness and grace, my wife, who was once a fundamentalist Muslim, came to the Lord. Many months earlier God had given me a promise, "Believe in the Lord Jesus and you will be saved, you and your household" (Acts 16:31). That day we worshipped together, "Praise to you Jesus, be glorified in all the earth".

On his arrival in Australia Daniel sought fellowship with Christians from Islamic backgrounds. In 1994 he commenced studies at Morling Bible College and completed the Diploma of Theology and Pastoral Ministry. He also has a PhD in International Management that he completed in Turkey.

# Introduction

Throughout history many people have remained ignorant of important truths relating to life. Leaders, writers and orators have often been instrumental in reinforcing such ignorance. Religious leaders are not exempt from blame.

There have been innumerable examples of religious leaders taking advantage of ignorant listeners and in this way making extraordinary political, social and economic gain through their manipulative and/or untrue messages. Historical evidence highlights the gravity of the situation when an ignorant leader comes to power.

The task of awakening people to the reality that they have been deceived has not been an easy one. Many people have lost their lives in the process of trying to do this.

I am convinced that, despite bans on free press and threats against advocates of free speech in many countries, we still have a responsibility to stimulate people to search for the truths concerning life. Mankind has been created with the potential to discover truth and to live in peace and unity.

My life in both Islam and Christianity, with all its pains and joys, has brought me to the stage of wanting to communicate my concern for truth. Blind adherence to leadership and traditions results from ignorance and breeds disunity and animosity amongst individuals and nations of the world. The material of this book is not meant to cause religious competition that takes advantage of ignorance but rather to open eyes and expose ignorance. Nor is it meant to produce hatred between people of different religious persuasions, but rather to provide a space for thought, evaluation and decision. Hatred is an impediment to discovery.

From the outset I want to say that every human life, whether enemy or friend, is precious. Indeed, I want to encourage the loving of others regardless of their rank, race, religion, nationality or other distinction.

The point of view expressed by any sacred writing will certainly have an impact on society, making it essential that the views are tested for the well being of that society and mankind in general. In some countries, ignorance is encouraged, and people are not free to read their sacred writings, preventing them from understanding and comparing their scriptures with other sacred works. Religious leaders are then free to interpret these scriptures for their own political gain legitimizing lying, stealing, killing, terrorism and similar activities. Such authority cannot be questioned, and coupled with ignorance has resulted in religious practices being imposed that are sometimes at odds with the original beliefs of the culture. Millions of people live under such control today. To move from such oppression, ignorance must be replaced by freedom to search and discover truth. We need to assist people to distinguish true belief from false so we can live together in peace with God and man.

Many people believe in war and enmity between people, but the human heart cries out for love and peace. A heart filled with peace radiates peace to those around. This is because the heart is the central tool in relationships with both God and humankind. If our hearts are in harmony with God, we will then become capable of loving others, resulting in peaceful relationships with God the creator and one another. God's love allows us to engage in relationships based on mutual respect, trust and reciprocal obligation. However, war and enmity between people produces a society characterized by unease and instability.

The nations of the world are in desperate need of loving hearts and for this to happen, we need to engage in a wholehearted drive against the spirit of enmity, war, ignorance and neglect of humankind. This directive can only take place through openness, sincere investigation and acceptance. As the need of people for a peaceful relationship with God and each other are met, they will put aside bigotry, fanaticism, nationalism and war.

Writing this book has brought mixed emotions. I have experienced tears, fear, courage, laughter, anger, patience, disappointment and hope at different times. But in the end, it has resulted in a sincere and pervasive inner confidence that the people of the world can be disarmed of any reason for division from each other. The hope of the Son was always with me throughout these experiences, strengthening me as I reflected on His unconditional love in my heart.

The overriding goal of this book is to provide a practical comparison of the Qur'an and the Bible by analyzing the impact of the teaching of each on the lives of mankind in all of its dimensions. My earnest prayer is that readers may discover the source of unconditional love and welcome the true and peaceful God into their lives. My hope is that they will become agents of peace bridging the walls of hostility between the peoples of the world.

# SECTION ONE:

## The Son

## The Son and Truth

We need to examine the Son because of His wise approach to the Truth. The way to the Truth is through knowledge and selection based on the exercise of free will rather than through coercion and imposition. He says, 'you will know the Truth, and the Truth will set you free'. The command "know the Truth" applies to all people throughout the world. Therefore, there are many reasons why the Truth must be discovered in the realm of the wider world. There could be some components in any faith that might work well for peoples' souls for a short time. But there is only one Truth in the whole world that always works for the utmost good and well being of the human soul. Truth is like medicine for the soul of mankind. Just as the most curative and potent medicine in the world is discovered as a result of its highly effective power in comparison with others, so the superiority and importance of Truth can only be proved through knowledge and comparison.

The Son points to universal Truth in order to join people of all nations under its uniqueness. Those who experience this Truth in their lives are set free from false dependencies and inhumane actions as they live a life of love.

In the mind and heart of the Son, hearing and obeying the truth is the solid rock, the safest place for building the life of humankind. It is strong and unshakeable in the face of any inhumane thought or claim or invasion.

Unlike other beliefs, the Son believes that the Truth itself must lead searchers to God, the source of Truth, and reveal Him to them in their life on earth. For the Son, God's kingdom starts on earth. So the revelation of Truth is the revelation of God Himself. In other religions, the greatest motivation to arouse interest in people towards the Truth is the revelation of God only in the life after death. Therefore, in other religions, the world is downgraded to be the 'no experiencing zone' and the 'no validation zone' for the Truth.

In the mind of the Son, those who initiate a mission to discover the Truth must have a purpose in doing so. The most convincing purpose for discovery is to experience and live the Truth. To live the Truth means to change through the newness and power of Truth and then to continue in the Truth through all of life. Therefore the Truth must change and take leadership over one's life on earth. In this way, the Truth reveals God into the lives of humankind in a practical way, transforming them into genuine godliness. Other religions do not acknowledge this practical aspect of the Truth.

Therefore, the philosophy of the Son regarding Truth involves providing a way for people to enter the Holy of Holies where humankind sees no veil between themselves and God. The Living God is then welcomed into all dimensions of life, making the knowledge of Truth practicable. In other words, if anyone is willing to discover the Truth, God, as the source of Truth, *will* reveal the Truth in a real and practical way. The Son wants people to be fully persuaded by the Truth as it relates to all dimensions of life. Then people will lay aside sin from their minds and hearts and dress themselves with God's Truth. The fundamental solution for being released from sin (Satan) is to meet the source of the Truth, God, who overcomes the power of Satan.

Once the Truth is discovered, the experience is one of walking hand in hand with God. No one is capable of describing or defending the Truth without the presence of God in their lives. One cannot be the messenger of Truth until set free by the Truth from all things in life that oppose it. Therefore, anyone who believes in the Son can live the Truth.

## The Son's Personality

The Spirit of this Son produces love, joy, peace, patience, kindness, goodness, faithfulness, gentleness and self-control. Because of His perfect holiness and goodness, He opposes immorality of any kind; impurity and debauchery, idolatry and witchcraft, hatred, discord, jealousy, fits of rage, selfish ambition, dissension, factions and envy, drunkenness, orgies and the like that damage human relationships. He can therefore bring a world of positive changes into the soul and heart of humankind and thereby into human societies. The Son is omnipresent, all knowing, the embodiment of goodness and completely inclusive in His love regardless of race, nation or religion. His purpose is to provide the means for humankind to be set free from the bondage of sin, ignorance, godlessness and false beliefs. In Him is found freedom from oppression.

His leadership is amazing. As the leader, He believes that a right condition must be provided to enable people to respond righteously. For this reason, He has devoted Himself to providing this right condition for all humankind to act righteously. This is found in the Kingdom of Heaven, the place God intends for the souls of humankind. He first encourages people to depart from the rule of sin and to enter the kingdom of heaven in this life on earth. In other words, He persuades people to change their citizenship from the kingdom of the ruler of darkness (Satan) to the kingdom of the Ruler of heaven (God). This is necessary because under the dominion of darkness, the conditions are all inhuman and therefore, no one is able to act righteously. Humankind must first be transferred into the right condition and clothed with the righteousness of the Son before the Spirit of God can bring about positive changes, which please God. The ministry of the Son is to provide the only means whereby people can be transferred to newness of life with God. The result of walking with God is seen in the ability to love, regardless of differences.

The Son believes that any person, including a prophet, who is not saved personally and has not tasted the joy of salvation in the presence of God, is not in a right condition with God, and so is precluded from being the messenger of salvation to others. A messenger must be one who has already been renewed through the experience of salvation and whose life exhibits the evidence of salvation. Such a person is in a position to evangelize others. Therefore the experience of salvation provides the way for people to live godly lives, serving others and leading people to God with open eyes.

Another amazing aspect of the Son's leadership is His humility. As He lived His life as a humble servant on earth, He demonstrated that humility was one of the greatest attributes for a leader. His humility was demonstrated as He cared for His co-workers by washing their feet in order to teach them how to love humankind. It was through His love and humility that He made salvation available for all nations. In Him, love and mercy triumphs over fighting and judgment. Those who are in Him are drawn to serve and love all humankind, including the enemy. His kingdom has no place for superiority; we are all of equal value in His sight and all become one through Him.

The Son's goal is to provide the right condition for reconciliation for those who carry the spirit of enmity toward humankind. This leads to friendship and oneness with God, fellow creatures of any race and color, and with nature. People who follow Him do not curse others, including their enemies. This leaves the door open for the Son's enemies to fall in love with Him and to serve Him. In His kingdom, we have confidence in the power of salvation and reconciliation and we can walk in heavenly places with Him.

He is unique in His nature and removed from the dualism of good and evil. He is purely good and is the beginning and the end of goodness. Compared to the dualistic foundation of Hinduism and Buddhism, it is evident that He is God of gods; compared to the foundation of Islam comes the realization that "O Lord there is none like You". Searching through all beliefs and ideas He is seen as the only One from heaven with the unique ability to reunite all people to heaven. Compared to the so-called peacekeeping minds and agents of the world, He is the Prince of peace and source of love for all nations.

## The Son's Clear Path to Salvation

Each religion subscribes to the idea of two final consequences for life after death; heaven (paradise) or hell, a joyful or sorrowful life, a good life or bad. One consequence seems pleasing to the souls of men and women in this world and motivates them to act according to their religion's criteria to obtain it, the alternative, however, is not pleasing. Rather it is terrifying, discouraging them from straying away.

In their lives on earth, people love to be certain that their destiny lies in heaven rather than the terrifying alternative of eternity in hell. However, no belief, except belief in the Son, is able to guarantee people the certainty of belonging in heaven. Uncertainty has permeated the foundation and teaching of other beliefs.

In the Son, the real issue of belief is the certainty of entering the kingdom of heaven. Through the Son people are given certainty about their individual status in the kingdom of heaven. There is no place for doubt when God's holy demands for right living are met through the Son. The Son is the only access to God and the Truth, as the sin that once separated us from the Holy God has now been laid on His Son.

## The Witness of the Conscience to the Son

The theology of the Son states that there is a witness or sign in the conscience of every individual in this world that can lead them to Him. The first part of this process is the implantation, by God, of the requirements of His law on the hearts of all humankind. The word of the Son says:

> *The requirements of the law (of God) are written on their (Gentiles') hearts, their consciences also bearing witness.* (Rom 2.15)

In creation, God breathed into us and made us living creatures. The breath of God carries along with itself into our souls the testimony and requirements of His law. The very message of the law of God in the heart says, 'I am your God and you are my people. I have created you for Me. Know your God and join Him otherwise you will be lost forever.'

The messages of God are simple and crystal clear to be discovered in every heart. Unfortunately, the majority of religions have introduced God to people in such a way that they are deluded into believing they are unable to discover the truths of the Creator themselves. They do not understand that they can and must be in personal relationship with Him in order to hear His testimony personally by their own consciences. Instead, many religions have introduced God as unreachable. They have brought people into a situation where they have totally lost trust in their ability to discover the truthfulness of God. As a result they have relied on the prescriptions and the mediation of their so-called spiritual leaders who have had a major role in spreading bigotry and ignorance. Such actions have contradicted the philosophy of the Son who points to the capability of any individual to discover the Truth.

When the need of the heart to be in relationship with God is discovered, through the conscience, then the person is convinced to allow God to meet that need. The heart moves forward, drawn by the attracting grace of the Creator.

Again, in the words of the Son:

> *So the law was put in charge to lead us to Christ.* (Gal 3.24)

In the philosophy of the Son, the first and real need of humanity is salvation, which means the joining of humankind to God during life on earth. The source of salvation is God Himself through His gift of a Saviour. God convinces the heart, through the conscience, that only He can save humankind. This process provides the individual with proof that humankind cannot be justified through their own deeds but only by their faith in the Son who has paid the ransom required for salvation. Men and women are chained and disabled through the bondage of Satan, sin, and they are unable to release themselves. They cannot overcome Satan. Only God can achieve this.

## A Personal Experience

The mission of the law of God, which points to salvation, can come to fruition in the heart of one who is willing to search for the Truth by evaluating and comparing the doctrines of various religions. Hearts need to be challenged with vital and simple apologetic, philosophical, logical questions about God and His Triune personality. This will enable people to critically evaluate the concepts and belief systems of a wide range of religions and judge which is the True way.

Another major purpose of this comparison is to evaluate the practicability of any message we hear and how it applies to all dimensions of life. The irreversible consequences of failing to achieve this are that it may prevent the formation of peaceful relationships with others and may lead our souls to eternal death. Humankind is created in such a way that if one does not search for the Truth and embrace it, one's soul will be lost forever.

## What is the Truth? Which Religion?

What or which religion is the True religion? Under what criteria can a religion be accepted as the True religion? What is the difference between the True and false religion? How can someone be sure of the suitability of the criteria used? What will be the consequence if someone is not aware of the falsehood of a religion and is taken in and misled by it?

Each religion makes a call upon people to accept its supremacy over others. For this reason, religious leaders have worked extremely hard to convince their followers to stay faithful to a particular religion. Each religion has a history of literature, having produced numerous books on discipleship in order to make more disciples to reach the world.

Each religion has established a specific theology to answer the questions of its followers and to encourage them to remain faithful to its traditions. Each religion claims to be the truest religion amongst others. Many followers have defended their claim at the cost of their lives. Many have suffered hardship, been imprisoned for long terms or endured life imprisonment for the sake of defending and living out their faith.

Considering the obvious or not so obvious differences, there must be one faith that is the most rewarding to the souls of humankind. To be able to make an informed decision requires investigation, understanding and comparison. Any religion or belief that encourages blind obedience does not allow a confidence in its followers that they are following the truest belief. It is my belief that investigating in this way will point out the superiority of the Son's philosophy.

## Revelation of Himself

A genuine religion should reveal God to His creatures. God is the Truth. So when God reveals Himself to man He reveals the Truth and casts away all doubt. There will no longer be any confusion as to which religion is The Way. Therefore, any confusion in any religion in this matter should raise questions as to its genuine nature. This manifestation of God on earth would also satisfy the nature of humankind's inner desire that longs to satisfy God and see Him face to face in this life or the afterlife. People know that God is superior to every other thing and that His words are superior to those of humankind. If He reveals Himself to humankind, this revelation would bring unity of faith and belief among the nations of the world.

So, the Son's criterion for true religion is to reveal God in the life of men, leading them to experience His revelation in their lives, have an intimate relationship with Him and be released of all uncertainty.

## Means of Reestablishing our Original State

For the Son there is only One God whose words and deeds are purely good. He is sinless by nature. Sin cannot be related to Him in any way. Therefore, the sinless God created sinless angels and a sinless man and woman with free will. In the beginning, the nature of Adam and Eve was sinless and only one of complete obedience to God. Sin found its way into their lives through an angel (later named Satan) who disobeyed God. This occurred when the angel misled Adam and Eve thus separating them from the company of God.

There are three basic steps for humankind to return to its original state with God:

1. The removal of the attitude of 'no to God' that carries the authority of Satan over humankind.

2. The establishment of the original attitude of 'yes to God' which the Son calls salvation or new birth or reunification with God forever.

3. The removal of the attitude of 'yes to Satan' (which produces sin, creating division amongst humankind through false beliefs and separation from God) and the establishment of a heavenly moral law in the heart of man.

A religion or belief can be judged true or false by its instructions about the way that humankind can return to its former state of unity with God.

Any religion that believes in humankind's self-sufficiency for releasing itself from the claws of Satan and returning to God is called false according to the criteria of the Son. The attitudes of 'no to God' and 'yes to Satan' have bound humankind to corruption. Human strength is neither above the power of Satan nor equal to the power of God. Therefore, they are unable to release themselves from the bondage of Satan and establish a just relationship with God. Evaluating the situation philosophically, the power of a life surrounded by the corrupt values of Satan is unable to establish a life that is purely good and pleasing to God.

Therefore, humankind cannot please God by what they do nor can they be with God through their own deeds. By their own strength, they are unable to gain freedom. There remains only one way that takes humankind home to be with God. It is through God's direct and personal intervention which removes the satanic authority over humankind in order to save them.

God is a personal savior who releases humankind from the bondage of Satan. This is the belief that only the Son holds, and it is He who establishes the True path for humankind. This True path allows man to walk into the Kingdom of Heaven and to be with God in this life and eternity.

On the contrary, other religions believe in the sufficiency of human strength for salvation. They do not believe in the necessity of the change required in an individual's spiritual identity. They ignore the fact that humankind is unable to overcome Satan since they have not been released from his dominion in their lives. In other words, Satan cannot be overcome by humankind when he has a place in their inner being. He has disabled all by sin. Therefore, there is none who can overthrow him by the power of their own deeds. We can only call on God to come reside within us in order to expel Satan out of our hearts forever.

As a result, humankind's spiritual identity needs to undergo a dramatic change from 'bad' to 'good' during their life on earth.    None but God can achieve this.

Considering all the above, the Son's philosophy for measuring the truthfulness of a religion or belief is simple. It comes down to whether the religion is able to release men and women from the bondage of Satan from now into eternity.

There are other values that can also be derived from the teachings of the Son that are all essential for discovering the truthfulness of a religion:

- As mentioned above, the True belief or religion must be able to plant the Spirit of God into the hearts and lives of people in a practical way and drive out the evil spirit. What I mean by 'practical' is that it must show the signs of life-changing power in one's life. In the philosophy of the Son, the dwelling of the Spirit of God in the heart is called the reconciliation of humankind with God and with each other on earth. When the Spirit of God dwells in the heart, He produces love, joy, peace, patience, kindness, goodness, faithfulness, gentleness and self-control, which all drive out the fruits of the evil spirit that separate people from each other and from God.

- True religion overcomes the heart through redeeming love and patience, not through brutality.

- As God has created men and women with free will, so must the True religion also respect the free will of any individual under the ultimate sovereignty of God. People must be given the opportunity to compare and evaluate in order to make an individual choice.

- There is real freedom in a True belief. A person not released from the bondage of the evil spirit is unable to consider the freedom of others in a realistic way since he himself is not free. Unless people are freed in their inner being, they will not be able to live out freedom in its fullest sense. The True belief gives freedom that generates peace and unity among people. It does not cherish hatred and passivity towards others, but instead love and kindness.

- The True religion has confidence in itself and therefore does not condemn those who make assertions against its values, making it open to world-wide criticism. It encourages respect rather than hatred. In the same way, the True religion does not impose itself on others.

- In order to be compared and evaluated with other beliefs and ideas, the True religion must be completely revealed to all.

- The True religion cannot claim a race or nation as better than others, knowing that all humankind originate from the same substance, dust.

- The True religion does not compromise by working with ulterior motives, but encourages honesty as the essential quality required in human relationships.

- The True religion comes to serve humankind by becoming a tool for a deeper understanding among diverse nations in order to remove the barriers separating them.

- The True religion must be God's blessing to all humankind. It is concerned for every one in the world and offers its love to all whether they be friend or enemy.

- The True religion allows people to scrutinize its leader's life. A true religious leader is the embodiment of truthfulness, setting a faultless example for all generations.

- True religion calls upon people make use of their own God given capability of analytical thinking, to examine the words of prophets and religious leaders, search for the best possible values in the world and choose the best with a free will. The truth cannot be discovered by blindly following or obeying the guidance of someone that has never been open to comparison or has never allowed it.

For the Son, the idea of many gods, or pluralism, fragments the world. Therefore, this cannot be a sign for a religion's truthfulness. A belief that divides the world cannot achieve the reconciliation that the nations of the world need in order to lead a life of peace and pleasure with one other. The unity of nations is the will of the Son's ministry. In Him, all the nations are able to break down the dividing barriers because of the unique love of the unique God. In this way, they can come into the unity of life and worship with each other in the kingdom of the One glorious God. The idea of several gods creates religious nationalism, which opposes reconciliation among nations. The Son rejects the worship of many religions and gods, not through fighting or putting down individuals and nations but through pure love. His love respects the rights of individuals and nations and, in this way, leads them to consider and to evaluate all values and in turn choose the best. His love is pure enough to draw every one in the world from other beliefs to Him.

A person who initiates the search for the Truth will most certainly discover it in the Son.

## The Message of the Son Is Also for the Muslim

There are three main reasons for supporting this claim:

1.  The law of the heart. God has imprinted the requirements of His law on the hearts of all mankind. This has already been discussed.

2.  Christians and Muslims are linked to each other in a specific religious way. Muslims believe that Islam is a continuation of Christianity. This requires them to be open with each other, accepting the truth that results from sharing thoughts and ideas in a very free and peaceful atmosphere.

3.  Christians and Muslims are also connected to each other as all are the descendants of Adam and Eve.

These reasons must challenge Muslims to act responsibly by not closing themselves off to hearing the Christian message. The major difference between the Qur'an and the Bible is the way the two beliefs have defined the truth and encouraged their followers to live out their religion. Therefore, the two beliefs must be compared and tested, in order to establish which makes sense. Muslims believe salvation is achievable through human deeds. In the same way, they believe that non-Muslims have to come to Islam, because they cannot achieve salvation through their own faith. These assertions have only been upheld in theory, not experience. The word 'achieve' is experimental in nature and is based on discovery and learning. Therefore, the universal claim by Muslims of achieving true faith must be accompanied by a willingness to exhibit Islam, without any fear, before a world of thoughts and ideas so that it can be compared and tested freely. Muslims need to let their faith be tested in all dimensions of life in order to prove whether or not Islam can be attributed to the True God.

The Muslim interpretation of the 'Son' has become a stumbling block for Muslims. They need to discover the meaning behind the Christian use of the word. For the Christian, the word 'Son' refers to God's plan of salvation. This might help Muslims to discover the freedom that is available for every person in the world through the Son, and to see Him as the fundamental means of gaining peace amongst nations.

# SECTION TWO:

# The Genesis of Islam

# A Brief Background

Muhammad was the founder of Islam. He claimed to be the prophet of Allah, who revealed his words (the words of the Qur'an) to him through the angel Gabriel. It is therefore instructive to consider his background and the experiences that shaped his life in order to make a comparison with the life and standards of the Son.

Muhammad first lived in the city of Mecca and was strongly influenced by the Jewish and Christian religious values that were widely spread in the peninsula of Arabia and the neighbouring countries. From Islam's early traditions, we learn that during Muhammad's youth in Mecca he had contact with Christians and learned much from their faith. He also met enslaved scholars from different religious and cultural backgrounds[1] who played a significant role in building his relationship with the Christian

---

[1] Muhammad-bin Jarir Tabari, *Tarikh-al-rosol val-molouk (The History of Prophets and Kings),* Tehran: translated from Arabic into Persian by Abolghasem Payandeh, Asatir Pub., 1996 (1375 Hijra), PP.1299-1302. & Ibn Hisham, *Sirat Rasul Allah, (The Life of Muhammad*, translation by R. E. Ibn M. Hamadani), Tehran: Ershad Islami Pub., 1998 (1377 Hijra), PP.189-192. . & N. Anderson, *The World's Religions,* England: Inter Varsity Press, 1994, P.93. & G. Nehls, *Christians Ask Muslims,* Nairobi: Life Challenge Pub., 1992, P.47.

churches in Mecca and Syria, and in building his theology.

However, it was at the age of forty when Muhammad called himself Allah's messenger. He said he had been sent to warn and guide the people of Arabia (c.f. Q.6: 92; 41: 44) and to call them to worship Allah[2]. He began preaching in Mecca around 610 AD and did so for about twelve years before migrating to Madina. Those who believed in the one God and accepted Muhammad as His messenger were called Muslims. 'Muslim' is an Arabic word that means 'one who submits' (to Allah) (c.f.Q.29:46c). 'Islam' is Arabic for submission.

## Factors which Influenced Muhammad to Undertake the Prophetic Ministry

### The Influence of the Poetic and Angelic Culture

Poetry is one of the oldest, most attractive and honorable ways of communication in all civilizations. Poets in every nation have won the

---

[2] Allah is the generic term for God in many middle-eastern cultures. Allah is identified as one of the 360 or so idols worshipped by the Arabian people for centuries before Muhammad was born. Many do not know that Allah was the moon god of the Arabians. This explains the crescent moon found on the minarets of mosques and the flags of Muslim nations. Historical writings also identify Allah with Baal.

respect of many people from generation to generation. Even hundreds of years after the death of some poets, the study of their poetry is kept alive through their followers. Some of them are promoted up to the level of prophethood by their followers because of their broad spiritual journey and discovery. Many people in the Middle East aspire to be poets, and in this way win the respect of their people. There is a common belief among people that a poet will never die in the mind and heart of the people. The poet's ever-contemporary words about life will always find eternal expression through the tongues of future generations.

In the Peninsula of Arabia, poetry was rooted in the mind and heart of the people and played a significant role in individual and tribal relationships long before the rise of Muhammad. The most successful poets gained the favor of people socially, politically, economically and religiously. It was a great joy to an Arab tribe when a poet appeared in one of its families. Celebrations were held for such an honorable moment, and people from other tribes joined the celebrations and congratulated the family and the tribe. Poetry was so important that whenever the families met each other, they wished each other the birth of a poet boy.[3] The life of a tribe was very much dependent upon warrior poets whose tongues were even sharper than their swords

---

[3] Read R. A. Nicholson, *Literary History of the Arabs,* England: Curzon Press Ltd, 1993 (first published in 1907), P.71.

in order to raise and strengthen the bravery of their members and to weaken their enemies.

Poets devoted themselves to guiding, looking after and defending the members of their tribe and to gaining glory for their tribe. All aspects of this responsibility were portrayed in the structure of the poems (ghasida, or qasida, and rajaz) and were recited wherever the situation made it appropriate. In times of war, poems were recited in order to recall the glories of past warriors and to weaken the spirit of the enemies by ridiculing, reviling and holding them up to shame.[4] In pre-Islamic culture, the purpose of the Arab warriors was not only to win the war, but also to gain glory for their tribe. The joy and glory of this victory led people to express the glorification of the tribe in poems and to pass that from generation to generation as a mark of honour to that tribe. This poetic language was common throughout the Peninsula of Arabia. Often, glorious stories of gods and heroes were told in this style to deliver the words quickly across the desert. In this way, attention was drawn to the messages.

Mecca, as the centre of shrines and religious poetry, played a significant role in spreading the poems through its many pilgrims to all parts of the Peninsula. Poems, though oral and unwritten, 'flew

---

[4] D. M. Lang (Editor), *Guide to Eastern Literature,* Great Britain: C. Tinling & Co. Ltd., 1971, P.3. & R. A. Nicholson, P.74.

across the desert faster than arrows, and came home to the hearts and bosoms of all who heard them'[5]. Poems were held more sacred when they portrayed the glory of gods who were able to protect their dependents from evil attacks. [6]

Muhammad was a clever Arab boy gifted in poetry and furthermore privileged by the many opportunities he received. After many years of travel and experience, he gained the courage to authorise the usage of commonly practiced and influential poetry as part of his ministry; a ministry of renouncing the lesser gods and praising Allah as the superior one of all. He grew up in Mecca and shared the excitement of the powerful poetic culture with his influential tribe, which was the custodian of the holy shrine, Ka'ba. A century before Muhammad, his tribe Quraish, rose to power in Mecca, multiplied its influence and thereby prospered socially, politically, economically and religiously. The Ka'ba attracted large crowds of pilgrims from all over the Peninsula. This not only increased the religious power of the Quraish, but also prospered them materially.[7] Muhammad, therefore, proudly carried the honour of his

---

[5] R. A. Nicholson, P.72.
[6] Read V. Bailey and E. Wise, *Muhammad: his times and influence,* Edinburgh: W & R Chambers Ltd, 1976, P.6. & J. B. Glubb, *A Short History of the Arab People,* London: Quartet Books, 1969, P.25. & S. Mackey, *Passion and Politics,* USA: A Dutton Book Pub., 1992, PP.31-34.
[7] Read R. A. Nicholson, PP.64-65.

influential tribe and practiced its religious customs wherever he went. Like his forefathers, he was interested in promoting religious acts in any way he could, whether it was idol worshipping, meditation at the Mount of Hira or the commonly accepted poetic recitation. The Qur'an also confirms that up to the start of Allah's call at the age of forty, Muhammad was considered 'lost' as a result of practicing the religion of his tribe (Q.93:7).

Poetic culture was very strong among the members of Muhammad's immediate and extended family. Prior to Muhammad's prophetic claim, his first wife Khadijah wrote very encouraging poems saying that she would enthusiastically wait for her beloved husband to announce himself as a prophet.[8] Muhammad's uncle, Abutalib, was also a poet. IIe wrote numerous poems about his nephew and sent them out to the public. He did this in order to gain the kindness of the people towards Muhammad, using this as a shield to protect his nephew against his opponents who wanted to hurt him. Abutalib's poems for the Ethiopian king, Nejashi, also show how influential poetry was at that time. These poems were written seeking protection for Islamic refugees in Ethiopia and they seemed more influential than the precious gifts of the leaders of Quraish, who wanted to persuade the king to return Islamic refugees from Ethiopia to their homeland Mecca.[9] The poetry prevailed and the king allowed

---

[8] Ibn Hisham, *Sirat Rasul Allah*, PP.169-72.
[9] Ibid., PP.245-50,315-6.

the fleeing Muslims to live in Ethiopia. Poems were used in every aspect of life and it should be noted that Muhammad and his followers never abandoned Arab poetic culture after the rise of Islam. Islamic traditions record many poems that were written for various occasions in order to strengthen the Islamic movement and also to weaken their enemies and opponents.

Arabian poets believed that no one could become an authentic poet unless a jinni[10], a spirit, appeared to him, possessed his soul and forced him to recite the inspired words of his mouth. Any who experienced the inspiring words of the spirits in such a way was highly respected by people. Muhammad spoke in a similar way about his revelation, saying that a spirit revealed the revelation to him and forced him to recite the inspired verses from his mouth. From the earliest beginnings of his ministry, he always wanted to include the religious values of his nation along with the beliefs of surrounding people. Not only did he say that the Jewish and Christian priests predicted his prophethood, but that the pagan priests also knew that he would be a prophet in the future. He asserted that every night Satan ascended to heaven, heard the latest news from the

---

[10] People believed that there were good and bad jinnis (spirits) both created by Allah from fire. They are powerful and intelligent creatures who serve the cause of Allah (cf. Q.15:27). Some Islamic theologians identify Satan with jinni and call him the head of jinnis (Read N. Geisler & A. Saleeb, *Answering Islam,* USA: Baker Books, 1997, P.37. & R. A. Nicholson, P.72).

spirits and came back to the pagan priests in Mecca and in this way spread the news among the people prior to Muhammad's claim.[11]

It seems that although Muhammad withdrew himself from his former religious practices, he kept his highly influential poetic and angelic beliefs, persuading people to believe in his recitations. These recitations were the verses of the Qur'an. Curiously, Muhammad did not call himself a poet (cf. Q.69:38-43) and even denigrated poets (Q.26:224-226) in his second Meccan ministry. Even though he did not consider himself a poet, the people regarded him as one because of the poetic style he used;

> *And* (people) *said, 'Shall we then abandon our god* (idols) *for a crazed poet?'* (Q.37:36)

Muhammad's attitude is astonishing as half of the Qur'an was recited in an Arabic poetic style.[12]

At the first revelation the spirit caught Muhammad forcefully and squeezed him so hard until his neck muscles twitched with terror. Muhammad felt as though he was being suffocated. He could no longer bear the pressure of the angel and therefore let the angel take control over him and make him repeat

[11] Ibn Hisham, *Sirat Rasul Allah,* PP.178-9.
[12] R. Tames, *The Muslim World,* London: Macdonald & Co., Ltd., Pub., 1982, P.16. & R. A. Nicholson, P.159.

his words.[13] Muhammad claimed himself to be a prophet due to such an 'inescapable' experience in order to convince people that his ministry was from above - authentic and irreversible.

## The Influence of the Followers of the "One God"

Muhammad's journeys, as a caravan trader, took him far from his home-town, Mecca, increasing his knowledge about the beliefs and lifestyles of other nations. This new understanding coupled with the strong relationships he had with knowledgeable religious people at home and abroad guided his revolutionary decision to reject idolatry and to worship the One God (c.f. Q.16:103; 6:105).

In Muhammad's time, two superpowers, the Byzantine (Roman) and the Sasanid (Persian) Empires had dominated different parts of the Arabian Peninsula, but Arabia was not a conquered nation[14]. Syria was in the hands of the Byzantine

---

[13] Ibn Hisham, *Sirat Rasul Allah,* P.209. & Read the narratives in Phil Parshall, *Inside the Community,* USA: Baker Books, 1994, PP.18-21. & K. Armstrong, *A History of God,* London: Heinemann Pub., 1993, P.161-3.

[14] B. W. Sherratt and D. J. Hawkin, *Gods and Men,* London: Blackie and Son Ltd, 1972, P. 74. & G. Wiet, V. Elisseeff, P. Wolff and J. Naudou, *The Great Medieval Civilisations*(Vol. III), London: George Allen and Unwin Ltd., 1975, P. 144. & Armstrong, PP.158-9. & V. Bailey, P.8.

Empire, while the Persian Empire ruled areas such as Iraq and Yemen. The Roman and Persian empires experienced six centuries of constant military, political and commercial rivalry that resulted in their domination of the above lands. However, the impassability of the Arabian Desert caused both empires to limit the operation of their armies to the central settlements of the area.[15] The only leverage that the West could rely upon in order to win the allegiance of the area was the evangelistic aspect of its religion, Christianity (unlike Zoroastrianism, the dominant religion of the East that did not believe in religious evangelism for reaching out to people). Therefore, Christianity played a significant role in the lives of the Byzantine ruled people. Christian missionaries were encouraged to reach out to the non-Christian communities wherever they could.

The Syrian Christians were also religiously and politically in favor of and in harmony with the Byzantine Empire. Therefore, the contemporary Church of Syria in Muhammad's time was trying hard to ensure that their contemporary Christian missions could flourish in Mecca and the surrounding areas. They realized that the Arabian businessmen were more interested in the Western way of life than in the Eastern way of life. Syrian Christians eagerly used this attraction to the Western way of life in their approach to Arabs. This also helped them to combat the activities of the

---

[15] J. B. Glubb, PP.21,23.

Nestorian Christians of Iraq who were in favor of the Eastern way of life and who had been trying 'to transmit the Aramaic Babylonian culture to all parts of the Peninsula'[16].

There were two ways the expansion of Christianity could benefit those Christians living under Persian rule; those living in Iraq[17] in the northern part of the Arabian Desert, in Yemen and in Nejran in the southern parts of the Arabian Desert.

Firstly, the influence of Christians in this area could be strengthened thus aligning themselves more with the Byzantine Empire, which in turn might expand this empire's dominion, freeing them from the Persian Empire's present and future threats and persecutions.

Secondly, they could easily identify themselves with the West as the centre of the Christian Empire, the source of Christian missionary effort and many other provisions as well.

From the time of his youth, Muhammad made various trips to Sham (Syria) accompanying his uncle, Abutalib, serving as a helper with his caravan. His close relationship with his uncle and Christians created a leaning in him towards the Catholic church. Because of this interest, he gained

---

[16] R. A. Nicholson, P.138.
[17] The majority of Christians in Iraq were of the Nestorian sect, which was called heretical by the Byzantine Church (J. B. Glubb, P.26).

favor with Bahira (or Buhaira), a priest from Sham, and with Nofel (or Naufal), a priest from Mecca. Nofel was a Hanifite[18] from Muhammad's own tribe, Quraish, who had converted into Christianity many years before the rise of Muhammad as prophet. Nofel was a notable Christian leader in Mecca, who was very old at the time of Muhammad's youth. Nofel arranged for Muhammad to work for his neice Khadijah, who was a widowed merchant[19]. He eventually married Khadijah. Through this marriage, he became more involved in religious matters relating to the One God. Islamic tradition says that Bahira, Nofel and Khadijah all knew that Muhammad would become a prophet and encouraged him to undertake the task.[20] After Muhammad received his first revelation, Nofel continually contacted Muhammad, confirming to him the revelation he had received and encouraging him to announce the prophecy. But, interestingly, Nofel's name is not among the names of those who became Muslim.[21]

Muhammad, therefore, was strongly affected by the contemporary Jewish and Christian belief of monotheism and this was one of the factors that influenced him to oppose the idolatry of Mecca.[22]

---

[18] Refer to footnote 29 for the word 'Hanif'.
[19] Ibn Hisham, *Sirat Rasul Allah,* P.168.
[20] Ibid., PP.158-61,168.
[21] Ibid., PP.210,214-32.
[22] Y. Armajani, *Middle East Past and Present,* Prentice-Hall, 1970, PP.30-31. & Riadh El Droubie, *Islam,* London: Ward Lock Educational Co., Ltd, 1983, P.7.

The teachers and the knowledgeable people who surrounded Muhammad also had a profound effect in shaping the future doctrine of Islam. One of the enslaved scholars who met with Muhammad was from a Zoroastrian background, and his name was Salman Farsi. Salman's part in laying the foundation for Muhammad's activities was highly significant.

Salman's life was an interesting one. He was a Zoroastrian from infancy and a magus highly experienced in the rituals and the beliefs of Zoroastrianism. However, while in his country, Iran, he went to a church in the city of Esfahan and became disinterested in Zoroastrianism in turn becoming more interested in Christianity[23]. He shared his view with his father. His father became furious and demanded him to cease any relationship with the church. Salman refused to comply with his father's demands. As a result, his father did not allow Salman to step foot outside the house. In desperation, Salman secretly sent a messenger to his Christian friends to ask if there was a caravan on

---

[23] We understand from Zoroastrian history that the Magi, who came to visit the baby Christ, were sent by the king of ancient Iran, Hormoz. The journey and the visit were given a valuable place in the religious memories and were considered as blessings to the land and people of Iran (The Yasna, book2 in Persian by Pourdavood, PP.167-172). This historical linkage between Christianity and Zoroastriansm might have been one of the reasons that Salman took refuge in Christianity.

route to Sham (Syria), a Roman state. He finally managed to escape to Syria and later served in the church. Throughout his Christian ministry, he visited some churches in Iraq, a Persian state. Afterwards he returned to Syria and at the advice of a prominent Christian leader he organized a journey to Arabia with the hope of seeing Muhammad in Mecca. (It seems that every church leader who spoke to Salman was trying to link Muhammad to the church.) On the way, he was assaulted and sold by the caravan drivers. His interest in visiting Muhammad might have upset the caravan leaders because Muhammad was speaking against their idols. As a result they decided to sell him as a slave. This led him to Madina, ruining his hopes of seeing Muhammad in Mecca. However, years after when Muhammad immigrated to Madina he released Salman who became a significant figure in the Islamic movement.[24]

Salman's various religious experiences created significant insight into Muhammad's mind when they spent time together. A comparison made in the following table proves how much Salman's knowledge and revolutionary background shaped Muhammad's religious-political life. The comparison between the historical foundations of Zoroastrianism and Islam brings forth the idea that, in all likelihood, Muhammad's revolutionary

---

[24] Ibn Hisham, *Sirat Rasul Allah,* PP.189-96. & Muhammad bin Jarir Tabari, *Tarikh-al-rusul val-molouk,* P.1301.

religious life was modeled on that of Zoroaster, the founder and the prophet of Zoroastrianism;[25]

[25] The following sources were used for the comparison between Islam and Zoroastrianism: Avesta: (Yasna, Gatha, Yashts, Visperd, Khordeh Avesta), research and translation into Persian by Hashem Razi, Forouhar Pub., 1995 (1374 Hijra), PP.19-20,26-28,33,230,370. & M. Rawlings, *Life-Wish: Reincarnation: Reality or Hoax,* Nashville: Thomas Nelson Inc., 1981. & M. Mueller, ed., *Secret Books of the East,* Oxford: Krishna Press, 1897-1910. & R. Cavendish, *The Great Religions,* London: Contact Pub., 1980, P.126. & J. A. Williams, *Islam,* Washington: Square Press, 1963, P.48. & J. R. Hinnells, *Dictionary of Religions*, Great Britain: Penguin Books, 1984, PP.361-2. & Hinnells, J. R., *Zoroastrianism and the Parsis,* Great Britain: Ward Lock Educational, 1981, PP..9,17,39,40,46,73. & J. B. Taylor, *Thinking about ISLAM,* Great Britain: Lutterworth Educational, 1971, P.27. & E. G. Parrinder, *A Book of World Religions,* Great Britain: Hulton Educational Pub., 1974, P.65. & The International Standard Bible Encyclopedia for Zoroastrianism. & R. Tames, P.27. & R. Zacharias, *Jesus Among Other Gods,* USA: Word Pub., 2000, P.190 (Footnote 3).

| **Muhammad** 570-623 A.D. | **Zoroaster** 569-492 B.C.? |
|---|---|
| He grew up at a time when his fellow Meccans worshipped many gods. | He grew up at a time when his fellow Persians worshipped many gods. |
| He was in relationship with some of the most knowledgeable individuals who lived at that time. | He was in relationship with some of the most knowledgeable individuals. |
| As he grew up, he spent much time meditating alone in mountain caves. | As he grew up, he spent much time meditating alone in mountain caves. |
| At the age of 40, he received a vision and following the first vision a second one that removed any doubt in him as being a prophet to win his countrymen away from the worship of many deities and win them to the service of one God. | At the age of 30, he received a vision and following the first vision other visions that removed any doubt in him as being a prophet to win his countrymen away from the worship of many deities and win them to the service of one God. |
| His first convert was his cousin (simultaneously with his wife). | His first convert was his cousin. |
| He had little success during his early ministry. The beginning of his success was when he traveled to Madina. | He had little success during his early ministry. The beginning of his success was when he traveled to Bactria. |

58

| | |
|---|---|
| His message at first was rejected and he was mocked and was forced to leave his hometown. | His message at first was rejected and he was mocked and was forced to leave his home. |
| He legitimised "holy war" (jihad) against idol worshipers and non-Muslims. | He legitimised "holy war"[26] against idol worshipers and later on his followers waged "holy war" against Christians mainly because it was the enemy's (Rome's) official religion. |
| Muslims with his guidance quickly destroyed the widespread idol worship and established their own belief in one God, a heaven and a hell. | Zoroastrians under his guidance quickly destroyed the widespread idol worship and established their own belief in one God, a heaven and a hell. |
| By his followers, He is called superior and incomparable to all humankind, in the perfection of his holiness. | By his followers, He is called superior and incomparable to all humankind, in the perfection of his holiness. |
| At one point in his | At one point in his |

---

[26] Zoroaster himself was martyred in the city of Balkh during a war launched by the king of Turan, Arjasb against his country (The Yasna; book 1, P.91 compilation and commentary in Persian by Pourdavood).

| | |
|---|---|
| prophetic ministry, Muhammad had a journey to heaven (cf. Q.17:1).[27] | prophetic ministry, Zoroaster had a journey to heaven. |
| Muslim prayers are said five times each day. | Zoroastrian prayers are said five times each day.[28] |
| Before praying, Muslims always wash ceremonially. | Before praying the Zoroastrian always wash ceremonially. |
| Prayers are recited in the language of the Qur'an. | Prayers are recited in the language of Avesta. |
| The corpse is washed and wrapped ceremonially prior to burial. | The corpse is washed and wrapped ceremonially prior to burial. |

Both Zoroastrianism and Islam believe that after death both righteous and unrighteous will enter hell. It is from hell that those whose good deeds outweigh their bad will pass over a narrow bridge, as thin as a single hair, and enter heaven. The unrighteous, though, will remain in hell.

---

[27] Ibn Hisham, *Sirat Rasul All,* PP.390-410. & Muhammad-bin Jarir Tabari, *Commentary on the Qur'an,* PP.1767-8.

[28] Day and night is divided into five, and each has its own specific prayer Avesta: (Yasna, Gatha, Yashts, Visperd, Khordeh Avesta), research and translation into Persian by Hashem Razi, P.370).

So, Islam was not only related to Christianity and Judaism, but to Zoroastrianism as well.

Muhammad's 'One God' idea was one of the other factors that caused him to take up the prophetic ministry. This idea attracted those Arabs who valued the worship of the One God like their ancestor Ishmael. It is obvious from the Qur'an that many Arab nationals believed in One God (Q.23: 84-90; 31: 25-26)[29]. In addition, we know from tradition that Muhammad's grandfather, Abdulmutallib, prayed to the *unique God* to protect Mecca from the invasion of Abraha, the governor of Yeman. Also, at the birth of Muhammad, he took the baby to the sanctuary and praised the *Almighty God* for his newborn grandchild.[30] Therefore, monotheism was not a revolutionary idea to the Meccan community. However, taking a stand against the idolatry rampant in Mecca was revolutionary.

---

[29] 'Hanif' was a religious group in the Arabian Peninsula, who proclaimed belief in one God, the God of Abraham, and rejected the polytheistic worship before the rise of Muhammad. They were neither Jews nor Christians but Arabs who were from Muhammad's own tribe, Quraish (R. Machatschke, P.3. & K. Armstrong, P.160: narrates from Muhammad's first biographer Ibn Ishaq). Muhammad called Hanifies the people of Abraham, and Abraham a Hanifite [Q.3:95; 4:125; 6:161].

[30] Ibn Hisham, *Sirat Rasul All,* PP.74-79,144. & Muhammad-bin Jarir Tabari, *Tarikh-al-rosol val-molouk*, P.708.

The early ministry of Muhammad, as the early writers of Islam[31] have pointed out, was not totally associated with the proclamation of the 'One God' idea. There were times in Muhammad's prophetic ministry when he exalted the three idols[32], al-Lot (goddess of fertility), al-Uzza (goddess of power) and Manat (goddess of fate) (mentioned in the Qur'an 53: 19-20[33]) by saying that they were divine beings assisting God (Allah) in his work. The exaltation of these idols was not in accordance with the philosophy of Muhammad's 'One God' ministry. Major set backs for Muhammad were the loss of his encouraging and loyal wife, Khadijah, and the loss of his uncle, Abutalib, who was like a shield for his

---

[31] Muhammad-bin Jarir Tabari, *Commentary on the Qur'an* (translated from Arabic into Persian 972-987 AD), Tehran: Tehran University Pub., 1977 (1356 Hijra), PP.1769-71. Muhammad-bin Jarir Tabari, *Tarikh-al-rosol val-molouk*, P.881.

[32] Al-Lot was worshipped by the tribe of Saghif who were from Taef. Al-Uzza was worshipped by the tribes of Quraish, Bani-Kananeh and Bani-Salim. Manat was worshipped by the tribes of Auss, Khazraj and Ghassan (A. M. A. Shahrestani, *Tozih-almelal (Almelal Valnahl),* Iran: Translated by S. M. Jalali-Naieni, Eghbal Pub., 1902 (1361 Hijra), P.386 of book?.

[33] These verses are known as *Satanic Verses.* After verse 19 in Q.53, the verse that exalted the three idols mentioned in verse 19 was, "These are the exalted females, and truly their intercession may be expected". Later it was replaced by the text as it now stands *(cf.* Q.22:51-52).

nephew.[34] Along with this he did not have any
influential political friends, who could shield him
from the political pressures that abounded at that
time. As a result he felt lonely and became more
vulnerable to his pain and the pressures brought on
by the unfriendly atmosphere created by the
Meccan leaders against him and his followers.
Because of this pressure he decided to make a slight
change to his political stance in order to gain the
favor of his opponents. To this end, he spoke in
favor of their idols and this in turn gained him the
ability to survive in Mecca for some years.

Nevertheless, this political stance in favor of idols
was not to last. In his later revelations in Medina,
when Islam was gaining more power, Muhammad
mentioned that there are some verses in the Qur'an
that were instigated by Satan with the permission of
Allah. He said that Allah was aware of them and
allowed them to be included in the pages of the
Qur'an initially, but now desired them to be
removed from the pages of the Qur'an by his
prophet;

> *Those who strive to invalidate our signs*
> *shall be inmates of Hell. We have not sent*
> *any apostle or prophet before thee,*

---

[34] P. W. Crittenden, *Islam,* London:    Macmillan
Education Ltd, 1972, P.7. & Muhammad-bin Jarir
Tabari, *Commentary on the Qur'an* (translated from
Arabic into Persian 972-987 AD for the fist time),
Tehran: Tehran University Pub., 1977 (1356 Hijra),
P.1689.

*among whose desires Satan injected not some wrong desires, but God shall bring to nought that which Satan had suggested. Thus God shall affirm His revelations for God is Knowing, Wise! That He may make that which Satan hath injected, a trial to those in whose hearts is a disease, and whose hearts are hardened. – Verily, the wicked are in a far-gone severance from the truth!* (Q.22:51-53).

Some people criticized him for the replacement of the already revealed verses of the Qur'an with the new ones. However, as is obvious from verse 51, Muhammad calls his critics unbelieving people who are destined for hell. In verse 53, he calls them those 'whose hearts are hardened' and therefore, they cannot accept that Muhammad can change the verses of the Qur'an. However, Ibn Hisham also asserts that those verses of exaltation that Muhammad said in favor of the idols were the words of his mouth but they were instigated by *Satan*.[35]

As mentioned earlier historical evidence shows that the word 'Allah' was the name of the great idol in Mecca, to which the forefathers of Muhammad offered their praise and honour.[36] The choosing of

---

[35] A. Guillaume: *'Islam'*, London: Penguin Books, 1954, P.189.

[36] R. Machatschke, *Islam: The Basics,* London: SCM Press Ltd, 1995, P.10.

the phrase *'Allah, the best creator of all'* in Q.23:14 might indicate that Muhammad's inner desire was to encourage his people to join him. By using a name they knew, and using it for the real God, he made a bridge for his people to cross from their old beliefs to belief in the 'best creator of all', Allah. This, he possibly thought, could attract contemporary Arabs to have an interest in Muhammad's call.

## The Effect of a Tolerant and Influential Tribe

A third factor that influenced Muhammad to undertake the prophetic ministry was his tribe. He was a member of Hashimi's clan, a dominant and influential tribe in Mecca called Quraish[37] that was the custodian of the sacred shrine of Ka'bah. The Hashimi's leadership in particular and the Quraishi's in general seemed much more tolerant towards those who converted into the One-God faith. This tolerance was because of their settlement in urban areas, having abandoned their nomadic way of life and being involved in trading with other parts of the world. Their relationship with other nations produced some cultural changes and flexibility compared to their primary Bedouin culture. As a result, some could dare to choose their preferred way of life, rather than hold rigidly to their old culture.

---

[37] Y. Armajani, PP.27-29.

Prior to Muhammad's acceptance as a prophet, there were people from the tribe of Quraish, some even from Muhammad's own relatives and friends, who took advantage of the tribe's tolerant leadership. They left the paganism of Quraish and joined the One-God worshipping group of Hanafi. One of them was the aforementioned Nofel, influential in the Christian church in Mecca[38]. Membership of such an influential and tolerant tribe provided Muhammad with a safe haven.[39] This enabled him to gain momentum so he could eventually follow a direction similar to his converted relatives and friends. Muhammad announced himself as a prophet sent to the Arabs and he soon grouped around him Arabs and slaves who were seeking to escape their paganism and slavery.

However, although the tribe was influential, there came a period of time when this influence declined

---

[38] In addition, there was Ubaydollah ibn Jahsh, Muhammad's cousin, Othman ibn Alhovaireth, who went to Rome and became a Christian, and Zeyd ibn Amr, who was the uncle of Umar ibn al-Khattab, one of Muhammad's father-in-laws, his closest companion and the second Caliph of the Islamic empire. It is said that Zeyd hoped to be sent as a prophet to the Arabs, and he opposed Muhammad's prophetic claim (Ibn Hisham, *Sirat Rasul Allah,*PP.198-202. & A. M. A. Shahrestani, *Iozih-almelal,* P.399 of book2. & K. Armstrong, P.160. & R. A. Nicholson (states Ibn Ishaq's comment), P.149-150).
[39] Muhammad-bin Jarir Tabari, *Tarikh-al-rosol val-molouk,* P.872. & Ibn Hisham, *Sirat Rasul Allah,*PP.414,418.

due to the death of those who provided significant support for Muhammad. As a result, Muhammad had no choice but to immigrate from Mecca to Medina.

## The Effect of a Scheming Wife

*Her wealth and links with Medina*

The fourth factor that influenced Muhammad to undertake the prophetic ministry was his marriage to Khadijah. Khadijah had strong trading links with cities like Medina and this marriage gained him great wealth and many Christian relatives and friends and provided him with a status consistent with that of a prophet. This great wealth financed his initial step to be a prophet and his new relatives strongly encouraged him, giving him confidence to continue his ministry.[40]

*Her Poems*

Muhammad's ministry was initially tough going. In the first three years after the first revelation, he felt as though he had been forgotten by Allah and even

---

[40] For further information read, Muhammad-bin Jarir Tabari, *Tarikh-al-rosol val-molouk*, PP.850-1. & Ibn Hisham, *Sirat Rasul Allah*,PP.158-61,168. & N. Anderson, P.94.

admitted having suicidal thoughts in his mind.[41] However, his faithful and insisting wife never left him alone and stood firmly beside him helping him to overcome his disappointments so that he could fulfill his prophetic ministry. Her poems to him were most encouraging, prompting him to take the prophetic ministry as seriously as possible and he made himself available for more religious preaching and activities.

## Her Persuasion

We learn from Islam's early reliable sources[42] that Muhammad himself was not able to distinguish the source of the voice that he first heard calling for him to be an apostle. He thought it possible that an evil spirit had possessed him. To be possessed by an evil spirit (Satan) was not strange or a thing to be detested according to Muhammad's cultural background. However, it was a serious issue for his wife Khadijah. According to the ancient Arabs, the best men of the tribes were those who were in league with and dependent upon evil spirits which an extraordinary role in bringing glory to the

---

[41] Read N.L. Geisler & Abdul Saleeh, *Answering Islam,* USA: Baker Books, 1997, PP.71,156. & B. W. Sherratt, P.78.

[42] Ibn Hisham, *Sirat Rasul Allah,*PP.212-3. & Muhammad-bin Jarir Tahari, *Tarikh al rosol val molouk,* P.851. & Muhammad-bin Jarir Tabari, *Tarikh-al-rosol val-molouk,* P.2034.

tribe.[43] This helps us to understand that Muhammad was not so much worried about being possessed by Satan, but was more concerned by his wife's reaction to the event. This assertion is supported by Muhammad's latter Meccan ministry, when he affirmed the belief of his forefathers calling the spirits (jinns or djinns) the servants of whom both Allah and his prophets were pleased with (cf. Q.34:12-13). When Muhammad shared with his wife that an evil spirit had possessed him, her immediate reaction was 'this cannot be, I have hope that you will be the prophet of these people'. She went to her uncle Nofel, the priest of the nearby church in Mecca, and recounted the story to him in order to obtain a view in line with her own. Having a political agenda, the priest believed it wise to share this view. As Khadija and Nofel were the two most powerful influences in his life, Muhammad was soon persuaded to claim himself as a prophet in Mecca. Nofel, the leader of the church in Mecca, was therefore the first person who gave approval to Muhammad's prophetic claim.[44]

## Fundamental Beliefs and Practices of Islam

### Fundamental Beliefs

---

[43] Read R. A. Nicholson, P.72. & Ibn Hisham, *Sirat Rasul Allah,*PP.178-81.
[44] Ibn Hisham, *Sirat Rasul Allah,*PP.210-11.

- Allah is the one true God. He is not of the trinity. Christians who believe in the trinity and say Jesus is God, are unbelievers and belong to hell for eternity (Q.9: 29-30; Q.66: 9).

- The Qur'an is the most holy book on earth.

- Muhammad is Allah's last messenger and his greatest prophet of all. Allah sent thousands of prophets and Muhammad is the seal of all.

- There are many angels and demons, and there is one Satan who deceives people.

- There will be a judgment day, and only on that day will people be able to find out whether they go to heaven or hell.

- Allah has predetermined the destiny of everybody before creation, be it in heaven or hell. People's righteous deeds may or may not effect the decision of Allah. Therefore, no Muslim is sure of personal salvation.

## Fundamental Practices

- Some of the practical obligations are prayer, fasting in the month of Ramadan, the pilgrimage to Mecca (Haj), paying alms.

- Every Muslim is obligated to pray five times daily (at sunrise, mid-day, mid-afternoon, sunset, and at night before retiring).

In regard to worship, Islam has followed an Arabian Jewish pattern of praying five times daily.[45] This also matches the Zoroastrian pattern of prayer that was mentioned in the previous chapter.

## Life and Death in Islam

- It is not easy to derive a clear statement regarding life and death in Islam. However, Muslims believe that life on earth is a period of examination in which every one prepares oneself for the life to come. The life in this world is a battleground between good and evil deeds. The predominance of good or evil deeds in this world will bring the relevant consequence after physical death - either eternal life or eternal death.

- Salvation or eternal life is based on continuous purification by good deeds in this world. Although each Muslim should try his

---

[45] Louis A. Ginzberg, *A Commentary on the Palestinian Talmud,* New York, Vol. I, 1941, P.73.

or her best to be good, ultimately God Himself will do the measuring at judgment day. Therefore in Islam there is no justification of sinners by faith as in Christianity, and no one, including Muhammad himself, is assured of personal salvation.

- Islamic people believe that God is just and will treat each according to one's deeds. However they traditionally, and without either logic or deep consideration of this, say that God may ignore their sins and forgive them. Therefore in this way, there is a false and even a non-Islamic hope among Muslims that salvation can be granted after death.

- Islam's heaven (paradise) is a garden with flowing streams, with beautiful greenery, fruits and maidens for men (Q.2: 25; Q.52: 22-23; 44: 51-55). 'These words are often described in pre-Islamic poetry; indeed it is highly probable that Muhammad drew a good deal of his teaching about paradise from this source.'[46]

---

[46] R. A. Nicholson, P.167.

# The Spread of Islam – Overview

At the end of his first twelve years of ministry, Muhammad's preaching severely angered the people of Mecca - some of them even plotted to kill him. The people of Mecca felt his ministry was not only spiritually a threat to their most respected shrine, Ka'bah, they also saw it as a serious threat to their peaceful relationships and trade, which were principles they felt obliged to uphold in honour of the deities in Mecca. The most hostile tribe of Arabia towards Muhammad was convinced that any kind of violence was dishonoring to the deities in the Ka'bah. Therefore, the Ka'bah was like a safe haven for all Arabs spiritually, socially, politically and economically. This was the reason why they saw Muhammad's message as a threat to all aspects of their lives and therefore tried to block his progress.

As mentioned previously Muhammad fled to Medina where his economic and religious affinities were very strong and there he was warmly welcomed. From this point of strength, he and his followers made raids on the Meccan caravans and this naturally encouraged hostility between them and his followers.[47] Ultimately, Muhammad and his followers returned to Mecca, occupied the city and forced the Meccans to accept Islam and to acknowledge him as prophet.

---

[47] Colin Chapman, *Cross & Crescent,* England, Inter Varsity Press, 1995, P.91.

After conquering Mecca and uniting the tribal leaders around him, Muhammad was heavily influenced by the Meccans. An outcome of this was that Muhammad became very nationalistic. He adopted some of the Arabic rituals that he had practiced before Islam. To satisfy the nationalistic desires of Arabs against Jews, he instructed Muslims to pray facing Mecca rather than Jerusalem (Q.2:142-144). It was at this time that he chose Mecca to be the holy shrine and the focal religious place for Muslims.

The hatred towards the children of Isaac was revived in Mecca at this time, even more intense than before the birth of Islam, since Jews and Christians started to reject and ridicule Muhammad's claims.[48] Muhammad turned his sword against the Jews and Christians, killing many both openly and secretly[49] calling it the battle of God against unbelievers;

> *Make war upon such of those to whom the Scripture have been given as believe not in God, or in the last day, and who forbid not that which God and His Apostle have forbidden, and who profess not the profession of the truth, until they pay tribute*

---

[48] W. E. Shephard, *Muslims Attitudes Toward Judaism and Christianity*, P. 2.

[49] Read Tabari, Muhammad-bin Jarir, *Tarikh-al-rosol val-molouk*, PP.997-8,1000,1056-7. Ibn Hisham, *Sirat Rasul Allah*, PP.491-3. & G. Nehls: quotations from the books of Sahih Muslim III PP.963-966.

*out of hand, and they be humbled. The Jews say, 'Ezra (Ozair) is a son of God'; and the Christians say, 'The Messiah is a son of God.' Such the sayings in their mouths! They resemble the saying of Infidels of old! God do battle with them! How are they misguided! (Q.9:29-30).*

In order to conquer the whole peninsula of Arabia, Muhammad took advantage of the many wars that occurred against various tribes and imposed Islam on them. In this way, the war against non-Muslims (jihad) became sacred in Islamic faith;

*Verily God loveth those who, as though they were a solid wall, do battle for his cause in serried lines! (Q.61:4).*

*O prophet! make war on the infidels and hypocrites, and deal rigorously with them. Hell shall be their abode! and wretched the passage to it (Q.66:9).*

Every Muslim by faith became obligated to take part in the war against non-Muslims [Q.2:216,217,253; 4:71; 8:65; 9:93-94].

The spread of Islam into other nations began with the invasions launched from Mecca and Medina. After Muhammad, his successors also encouraged holy war (jihad) against non-Muslims. Some Christians also welcomed the spread of Islam as it helped them to become free from Byzantine rule.

One example of this, was the Copts in Egypt who joined forces with the Muslims to drive out the Byzantine.[50]

Muslims conquered large portions of the two existing Empires, the Byzantine and the Persian, within a single decade. One after another the nations of Israel, Syria, Mesopotamia, Egypt, Iraq, and Iran were conquered with the power of the Muslims' sword. Muslims continued conquering as many nations as they could and built an Islamic empire that stretched from northern Spain to India.[51]

## Insights into Muhammad's Political and Religious Thinking

Before his emigration to Medina, the 'spirit of war' was silent in Muhammad despite all the pressures on him. But after he fled from Mecca to Medina and founded a stronger following there, he suddenly turned his assembly into a fighting group. He did this in order to prevail against his opposition in Mecca. His strategy was to first invade the Meccan caravans and then the city itself. Unlike the pagan Meccans who valued the month of Ramadan and would not initiate any war against their enemies in

---

[50] A. M. A. Shahrestani, *Tozih-almelal,* P.39 of book1. & Colin Chapman, P. 128.
[51] F. Quilici, *Children of Allah,* USA: Chartwell Books Inc., 1978, P.70. & C. Chapman, P.9.

it, Muhammad ordered his followers to attack unarmed caravans even in the so-called sacred month of Ramadan (Q.2:217)[52].

Medina was geographically well placed between Mecca and the Mediterranean world to cut the caravan route, which was of vital importance to Meccans' lives.[53]   Under Muhammad's leadership, Muslims made much plunder from the raiding of caravans and from the battlefield.[54]   One fifth of everything that was gained in war belonged to Muhammad, his families, orphans and the poor. The remaining four-fifths was to be divided among the warriors.[55]   This encouraged Muslims to take revenge for what the Meccans had previously done to Muhammad and his followers. In this way, the warlike spirit of pagan Bedouins[56] was not rejected by Muslims, but instead revived by Muslims more than ever before.   Muhammad used the Bedouin strategy to empower the decision of his followers to fight and to gain the victory. The explosive force of the nomad world was linked to the preaching of Muhammad and a relationship of mutual help and dependence developed.[57] This mutual dependency

---

[52] This verse of the Qur'an contradicts the verse Q.9:5 which does not encourage war and killing in Ramadan.
[53] J. B. Glubb, PP.34-35.
[54] Read: Muhammad-bin Jarir Tabari, *Tarikh-al-rosol val-molouk*, PP.933-40,944,945, 950,1007.
[55] Ibid, P.998. & V. Bailey, PP.18-19.
[56] K. Savage, *The History of World Religions,* London: The Bodley Head, 1970, P.118.
[57] F. Quilici, P.68.

gained power for Muhammad and prosperity in the form of wealth and possessions for his followers. The political aspirations and decisions of Muhammad and his companions were offered to the community as the inspired verses of God, which could not be reversed or rejected. The atmosphere that Muhammad created was quite different to what Jesus created for people. Jesus, unlike Muhammad, offered a journey of thought that brought people into a dramatically different way of living and thinking from the way they were accustomed.[58] The spirit of war that was upon the people in Medina did not allow them the time to take Muhammad's preaching into their inner beings and evaluate them. Who was able to speak logic with the sword? People were so caught up with the rush and force of war that they did not have the chance to think or evaluate. Therefore, the people in Medina failed to consciously evaluate whether the verses of the Qur'an could be attributed to God or not. However, some people realized the problem and started blaming Muhammad. Muhammad took their criticism as a real threat to Islam and therefore launched a systematic plan to exterminate his critics from society. People had no choice other than to obey him because the Qur'an stipulated that his commands were to be considered as equal to God's commands (Q.33:36).

---

[58] Read R. Zacharias, PP.29,46.

## The Cause of Disinterest in Islam

Clearly, Muhammad was himself the cause of some of the criticisms that people made against him. His unstable beliefs expressed in the Qur'an (or the new religion) led to critiques being raised against him. On one hand he says that the followers of other religions need not feel saddened by the prospect of hell because no fear will come upon them. On the other hand, he expresses a contradictory attitude when he claims that Islam is the one and only. Examine the following passages;

> *Verily, they who believe* (Muslims), *and they who follow the Jewish religion, and the Christians, and the Sabeites - whoever of these believeth in God and the last day, and doeth which is right, shall have their reward with their Lord: fear shall not come upon them, neither shall they be grieved* (Q.2:62).

On another occasion, he said that the book given to Moses was complete and was a means through which people could meet their Lord;

> *Then gave we* (God) *the Book to Moses - complete for him who should do right, and decision for matters, and guidance, and mercy, that they might believe in the meeting with their Lord* (Q.6:154).

People could say: if the followers of other religions have been freed from fear and if the book given to

Moses lifts the fallen people up to the presence of their Lord, why will they be in need of a new religion?

At another stage in his life, Muhammad said that he is not an upstart among the messengers of Israel, but the one who testifies something similar to what the children of Israel testified;

> ...I am no apostle of new doctrines...this book[59] be from God... its conformity with the Law (Q.46:9-10).

This statement of doctrinal similarities, of course, was not confirmed by Jews and Christians who knew the central theme of their book, the Bible. Therefore, they started mocking and rejecting him as the Qur'an even records;

> ...they said, 'This is manifest sorcery!' (Q.61: 6).

Either Muhammad's exaltation of idols at one time (as was mentioned earlier in this book) or his own doubts about the Qur'an could also have been cause for people to ridicule him. As a result, these people avoided joining his movement;

> And if thou (Muhammad) art in doubt as to what we have sent down to thee, inquire at those who have read the Scriptures before thee. Now hath the truth come unto thee

---

[59] The Qur'an.

*from thy Lord: be not therefore of those who doubt. Neither be of those who charge the signs of God with falsehood, lest thou be of those who perish* (Q.10:94-95).

The pressure of multiple opponents brought Muhammad to such a point that he intended to give up Islam. He reflected to others that the reason for this was his doubt in Islam. Therefore, his own decision to give up Islam and his doubts about Islam would certainly have caused many people to be disinterested in Islam. But then a radical change occurred in him. Soon afterwards, when he gained power, he forced people to come to Islam and killed those who did not come to believe in it. This is the saddest and the most painful part of humanity. How tragic when people must be sacrificed because of a leader's uncertainty!

As further evidence of this uncertainty, look at what Muhammad said about Christians. On one hand he said the followers of Jesus Christ are ahead of unbelievers until the day of resurrection and in this way he indirectly guided Christians to stick to their religion and stay firm in their faith;

*... God said,...I will place those who follow thee* (Jesus) *above those who believe not, until the day of resurrection* (Q.3:55).

On the other hand, he forced them to believe in Islam and to follow him;

*Make war upon such of those to whom the Scriptures have been given as believe not in God, or in the last day, and who forbid not that which God and His Apostle have forbidden, and who profess not the profession of the truth, until they pay tribute out of hand, and they be humbled...The Jews say, 'Ezra is a son of God'; and the Christians say, 'the Messiah is a son of God.'...God do battle with them! How are they misguided (Q.9:29-30).*

Why would a Christian nation, who has overcome the sin of disbelief, be forced to change their faith? Isn't the victory over disbelief called the victory over Satan? If there was no doubt that Christians were winners through Jesus Christ, why would they leave their victorious King and come to join Muhammad who had no assurance in his own ministry? Needless to say, the unstable and shifting position held by Muhammad has caused severe havoc for Christians ever since the beginning of political Islam.

Muhammad killed many people, expelled the Jewish tribes from Medina, and seized all their property.[60] The forefathers of these Jews had fled

---

[60] Read: Muhammad-bin Jarir Tabari, *Tarikh-al-rosol val-molouk*, PP. 997,998,1006,1056-7. & Ibn Hisham, *Sirat Rasul Allah*, PP.491-3. & W.M. Watt, *Muhammad at Medina*, Oxford: Clarendon Press, 1956,P.14-16. & M.H. Haykal, *The Life of Muhammad*, Indianapolis:

from Roman persecution in Jerusalem centuries ago.[61] Through the centuries of hard work, their generations had built their lives in Medina, surviving the ages of violence, lawlessness and idolatry in the Peninsula of Arabia.[62] Obviously, the town of Medina owed much of its prosperity to the highly skilled Jewish inhabitants.[63] However, it is distressing to see that under the government of the so-called civilized Islam they were not even given a chance to live. In one of his attacks on the last Jewish tribe in Medina, Muhammad called the Jews the sworn enemies of Allah, killed all the men of the tribe and sold the woman and children into slavery.[64] Those of his opponents, who escaped and took refuge in Mecca, were killed or forced to accept Islam by Muhammad when he later captured Mecca. So, in this way, the prophetic calling of Muhammad turned into a dictatorship with many battles and the shedding of blood occurring after his emigration to Medina.

---

North American Trust Publications, 1976, P.243-4,278. & J. B. Glubb, PP.35-36.

[61] P. W. Crittenden, P.4. & K. Savage, PP.124-5.

[62] Muslims call the pre-Islamic Arabs ignorant (jahil), lawless, violent and idolaters (J. R. Hinnells, P. 168 & R. El Droubie, P.5).

[63] P. W. Crittenden, P.4.

[64] T. Andrae, *Muhammad: The Man and His Faith,* New York: Harper & Row Publishers, 1955, PP.155-6.

## The One Community of Hezballah

After his emigration, it was not a kind of theology that ran the course of Islam but a fighting and fluctuating spirit against flesh and blood, although Islam carried with itself various religious rituals too. This agenda was driven by a conviction that 'the region must be conquered by the sword' in order to rescue the world from corruption;

> ...and were it not for the restraint of one by means of the other, imposed on men by God, verily the earth had been utterly corrupted (Q.2:251b).

In this way, Islam became the first and last religion ever in the history of humankind that believed so extremely in erasing the believers of other religions at all times and in all places. Indeed, the harshest pre-Islamic cultural values were all gathered from the various tribal values and united into, what seems to be, a single tribe of Islam, Hezballah, which must overcome all other so-called corrupt groups. In other words, the habits and cultural values of the conquerors became the dominant and authoritative forces over the region. All tribes were forced in absolute dedication to Muhammad as the chief of the new movement, which meant no one had freedom of choice in any of their affairs (Q.33:36).

Muhammad's bloody battles were in huge contrast with his earlier ministry. 'In Mecca he had been the rejected prophet but in Medina he soon became statesman, legislator and judge - the executive as well as the mouthpiece of the new theocracy.'[65] In his earlier ministry in Mecca, he relied very much on a prophetic culture, which was a calling of people to fear the true God. Contrary to his earlier ministry, his later ministry became predominantly legal and political, and he relied on forcing people to follow him. He invaded tribes by the thousands and forced them to follow him as the head of the state religion. In his earlier ministry, he was harmless to idol worshipers and friendly to every one who believed in one God. However, in his later ministry he called any who did not follow him an enemy, no matter if the person had faith in one God or many gods. It was from this time that many contradictions in the verses of the Qur'an began to appear.

After his emigration to Medina, everybody had to please Muhammad by giving up his/her religion and following his instructions. This was because he was no longer a rejected prophet, but a powerful political figure with the goal of turning the various religious and cultural ethnicities in the Peninsula of Arabia into a single community of Islam, Hezballah. He then decreed;

> ...it is not for a believer, man and woman, to have any choice in their affairs, when God and His Apostle have decreed a matter: and

---

[65] N. Anderson, P.95.

*whoever disobeyth God and His Apostle,*
*erreth with palpable error* (Q.33:36).

If someone, for any possible reason, did not live to please the prophet of Allah, he/she would be brought face to face with the sword. The authority he laid over his people was even more than a contemporary bedouin chief possessed over his tribe.[66]

So, in this way, the growing doctrine of Islam became subject to influence by the Muslim strategy of non-stop invasions of other peoples and tribes;

*...kill those who join other gods with God*
*wherever ye shall find them: and seize them,*
*besiege them, and lay wait for them with*
*every kind of ambush: but if they shall*
*convert, and observe prayer, and pay the*
*obligatory alms, then let them go their way,*
*for God is gracious, Merciful* (Q.9:5).

Invasions and forcing people to believe in Islam became the climactic issue of Muslim doctrine. In order to make the growing body of doctrine convincing Muhammad welcomed all sort of ideas that could give the movement a religious flavour. This kind of politics, especially when it is accompanied by force, has always been convincing to nominal people under threat, throughout history. When people see themselves face to face with death,

---

[66] P. W. Crittenden, P.12.

more often they prefer to choose life with whatever conditions the dominant power imposes on them. This was what happened in the Arabian Peninsula as well. Muhammad and his companions forcefully convinced people that his invasions were God's will and ought to be accepted as an expression of irreversible religious values. Therefore, Islamic doctrine couldn't help but contain the words and acts of a group of fighting warriors and this was presented to others as the absolute law that must be obeyed and honored. Thus, a fighting spirit became the leading characteristic in producing the doctrine of Islam. The battles against Meccans turned into battles against non-Muslims and ultimately swept through entire societies that were full of a variety of people, including Christians and Jews.

Muhammad's views became subject to the enormous growth in his political power and this is seen clearly in the changing ethics applied in the treatment of Jews and Christians. The Qur'an clearly reveals two opposite views about Jews and Christians that were held at different times. The verses of his early ministry were apparently in favor of Jews and Christians and consequently in favor of biblical theology, but the verses after his emigration were against the followers of the Bible and thus contrary to biblical theology.

# The Cause of Instability in Friendship

When a doctrine becomes subject to war, it undoubtedly contradicts itself in many ways. A fighting spirit always searches for full armor and empowerment, no matter what it will cost the community. This is the major aim in fighting. To do so, the warring authorities sometimes decide to stay in favor with a particular group and out of favor with another. Subsequently, though, because of a change in war policy, they change their strategy and become friends with their previous enemy in order to crush their previous friend. Such an unstable spirit always ends up opposing its own doctrine in many areas. That is why the Qur'an contradicts itself so many times. For example, in regard to the prophetic role of Muhammad Allah states that Muhammad's ministry is not to lead people but to call them in a peaceful manner, since man is alert and able to distinguish the good from bad. On the other hand, Allah commands Muhammad to fight people and frighten them until they come to Islam and offer their allegiance to it (cf. Q.76:2-3; 2:272; 3:19-20,110; 22:49; 9:29).

In this way, the so-called theocratic law of Islam imposed on people an unstable standard, in which no one could ever hope for a long-term friendly relationship with each other.

This bitter, fearful, painful and hopeless instability cannot be attributed to the loving and merciful God who desires and calls people back to heaven as the place of peace and honest relationships.[67]

The instability of relationships in Islamic politics has reduced the level of sincere mutual trust among people and as a result has caused many to spy on one other in fundamentalist Islamic societies. Many force themselves into a situation where they have to be two-faced. This unrealistic life sometimes penetrates into the inner world of families and of immediate friends, bringing with it many unfortunate results. For example, the disagreement between the successors of Muhammad and the war between Muhammad's beloved wife, Aysha and his beloved son-in-law, Ali, were the result of Muhammad's own fluctuating values with respect to relationships. The members of his own family and state became a threat to each other.

In this way, sincere family fellowships were changed into an impossible situation for many. Even mothers, who are known to be a source of shelter and trust for their children, became yet another threat to the members of their family. After the revolution in the Islamic Republic of Iran, several mothers were rewarded as being pure Muslims when they surrendered their children for the crime of following other Islamic leaders rather than the Ayatollah.

---

[67] Read the Gospel of Jesus Christ.

## Interest in the Objects of Pagan Faith

Muhammad originally had Christian companions. Later on, people who had previously opposed him became his companions as they desired a religion that was oriented around and for Arabs. The pure biblical thoughts that were once honored by Muhammad were no longer suited to his new surroundings. In his early Meccan ministry, when he was highly affected by Christian thought, he called on God to guide him on the straight path, which is the path followed by Christians and Jews;

> *Guide Thou us to whom Thou hast been gracious; -with whom thou art not angry, and who go not astray* (Q.1:7).

This belief, however, did not stay the status quo for long. Now pagan religious rituals were to be adopted and incorporated into Islam;

> *Verily, Safa and Marwah are among the monuments of God: whoever then maketh a pilgrimage to the temple, or visiteth it, shall not be to blame if he go round about them both...* (Q.2:158; cf. 22:26-27).

The hills of Safa and Marwah in the above verse are in the sacred territory of Mecca, and these had been the objects of pagan worship.[68]

---

[68] Read the note number 62 in THE KORAN, translated by J. M. Rodwell, London: Everyman, 1994, P.435.

In the early years of his ministry, Muhammad had no interest in the objects of pagan faith. However, the pro-Arabic nature of his later ministry not only resulted in the revival and legitimization of some of these pagan rituals[69], but he also called Jews and Christians, who believed in One God, to leave their biblical path and instead follow his newly adopted path. Although his path became quite different to that of Moses and Jesus, he still wanted Christians and Jews to make no distinction between himself and other prophets. Those who did make a distinction and even those who desired to take a middle way were all made subject to shameful punishment;

> *Of a truth they who believe not on God and his Apostles, and seek to separate God from his Apostles, and say, 'Some we believe, and some we believe not,' and desire to take a middle way; These! they are veritable infidels! and for the infidels have we prepared a shameful punishment. And they*

---

[69] Muhammad sanctified and dedicated the ancient pagan shrine, Ka'bah, to Allah and Islamised the pilgrimage of 'Hajj' to it. The pilgrimage of 'Hajj' was one of the most respected pagan rites and he made it the 'fifth' pillar of his religion (Read Tabari, Muhammad-bin Jarir, *Commentary on the Qur'an*, P.1771. & H. Thomas, *An Unfinished History of the World,* London: Hamish Hamilton, 1979, P.145. & K. Armstrong, P.182 & K. Savage, P.125 & B. W. Sharratt, P.76).

*who believe on God and his Apostles, and make no difference between them - these! we will bestow on them their reward at last. God is Gracious, Merciful* (Q.4:150-152).

People were not given any freedom to compare and choose the best belief that represents a high quality of life and faith. Instead, blind submission, obedience and allegiance became the lasting focal points of Islam. Every one was forced to confess faith in Muhammad. This led Muslims after Muhammad to build their theological foundation simply on the two rigid confessions, 'there is no god except Allah, and Muhammad is his messenger'. These two statements were announced to the world, not for open evaluation and selection but as forceful 'gifts' from Islam requiring blind submission by the world. Any act of objecting to Muhammad was taken as an objection against God and therefore carried the death penalty with it. According to Islam, if Allah has revealed that Muhammad's will must be done on earth, then how could the people of the world dare to ignore or oppose his will?

# SECTION THREE:

# The Author of the Qur'an(Koran)

# The Copy of the Original Qur'an

Muhammad's associates preserved his teachings by memorizing or writing them down during his lifetime. Later, the materials of his teaching were collected and made into a book, called "the Qur'an" (Koran). The word "*Qur'an or Ghur'an*" means "*reading aloud or recitation*" which is derived from its Arabic root "*qara'a or ghara'a*", *meaning "to read*". The first word "*eqra or eghra*" (the command form of the verb "*read*") that Muhammad heard from the angel might have been one of the reasons for Muslims to name their holy book "*Qur'an*" which is from the same root as "*eqra*".

Muslims believe that the Qur'an is the pre-existent, eternal and authoritative words of God inspired by the angel Gabriel to Muhammad, in order to be recited in Arabic to Arabs. They believe that it is God's full, final and supreme revelation given to Muhammad throughout some twenty-three years of his ministry;

> *Elif. Lam. Ra. These are signs of the clear Book. An Arabic Koran have we sent it down, that ye might understand it* (Q.12:1-2).

> *Ha, Mim. By the Luminous Book! We have made it an Arabic Koran that ye may understand. And it is a transcript of the archetypal Book, kept by us; it is lofty, filled with wisdom* (Q.43:1-4).

*Recite thou, in the name of thy Lord who create; Created man from CLOTS OF BLOOD; Recite thou! For thy Lord is the most Beneficent, Who hath taught the use of pen; Hath taught Man that which he knoweth not* (Q.96:1-5).

*SAY: whoso is the enemy of Gabriel - For he (Gabriel) is who by God's leave hath caused (the Qur'an) to descend on thy (Muhammad) heart, the confirmation of previous revelations, and guidance, and good tidings to the faithful* (Q.2:97).

The word "Recite" in Q.96:1 means the recitation of those words that were already written and existed.

For Muslims, the Qur'an supersedes any other religious books in the world. According to Islamic faith, no one else's thoughts, including Muhammad's, could be reflected in the Qur'an, because it is a copy of the original Qur'an, which is in heaven;

*What He pleaseth will God abrogate or confirm: for with Him is the source of revelation*[70] (Q.13:39).

---

[70] In Arabic, the 'source of revelation' is 'Om-al-Kitab', which literally means 'the Mother of the Book' or the Qur'an.

*Thou didst not recite any book (of revelation) before it: with that right hand of thine thou didst not transcribe one: else might they who treat it as a vain thing have justly doubted: But it is a clear sign in the hearts of those whom 'the knowledge' hath reached. None except the wicked reject our signs* (Q.29:48-49).

*Yet it is a glorious Koran, Written on the preserved Table* (Q.85:21-22).

## Authenticity

However, the Qur'an's own verses and Islam's own ancient authentic sources[71] do not support it as being the pre-existent, eternal and the authoritative word of God. Credence is given to the contribution of other writers to the Qur'an, as many verses in the Qur'an are not inspired through Muhammad but are from his companions.[72]

The present Qur'an was also called incomplete and different from other rival versions and was accepted as false by many eye witnesses of Muhammad –

---

[71] For example; Muhammad-bin Jarir Tabari, *Tarikh-al-rosol val-molouk*, P.882. & Muhammad-bin Jarir Tabari, *Commentary on the Qur'an*, PP.1769-71.

[72] A. Dashti, *Twenty Three Years*, London: George Allen & Unwin, 1985, PP.98,111.

even by Muhammad's own son-in-law, Ali, the first holy leader (Imam) of the sect of Shia.[73] According to the old authorities and Hadiths[74] of Islam, there were many disagreements amongst the contemporary followers of Muhammad over the wordings and readings of the Qur'anic verses. Muhammad himself became uncertain and could not recognize the original words and readings. Therefore, he ordered each one of his followers to follow whatever scriptures they had, regardless of the differences in the meanings and versions.[75]

He had also claimed that the Qur'an can not be inspired by anyone besides Allah;

> *And if ye be in doubt as to that which we*
> *have sent down to our servant, then produce*
> *a Sura* (chapter) *like it, and summon your*
> *witnesses, beside God, if ye are men of truth:*
> *But if ye do it not, and never shall ye do it,*

---

[73] G. Nehls, PP. 52-55.

[74] Hadiths are the writings about Muhammad's and his companions' sayings and deeds, which guide Muslims in founding their social laws and governments, and also in conducting their daily lives (cf. Q.4:80; 7:157; 14:44;33:21). Sometimes Muslims regard the writings of the Hadiths on a conditional basis. They do not welcome those parts of the Hadiths that represent contradictions. To evade the contradictions, they rather rely on their own notions. However, without referring to Hadiths, Muslims are not able to discover the original context of the words spoken by Muhammad; the time and the occasion they relate to.

[75] G. Nehls, PP. 57-65.

> *then fear the fire prepared for the infidels, whose fuel is men and stones (Q.2:23-24).*
> *Can they not consider the Koran? Were it from any other than God, they would surely have found in it many contradictions (Q.4:82).*
>
> *Moreover this Koran could not have been devised by any but God... Do they say, 'He hath devised it himself?' SAY: Then bring a Sura like it; and call on whom ye can beside God, if ye speak truth (Q.10:37-38).*
>
> *SAY: Verily, were men and Djinn[76] assembled to produce the like of this Koran, they could not produce its like, though the one should help the other (Q.17:88).*

Muhammad again had claimed that the Qur'an was an inspired revelation to him with the full knowledge of Allah. He purported that Allah and his angels were witnesses to this, and none could change it, and that he was merely a mouthpiece for the inspired words of Allah;

> *But God is himself witness of what he hath sent down to thee: In His knowledge hath He sent it down to thee. The angels are also witnesses: but God is a sufficient witness (Q.4:166).*

---

[76] Spirits.

*Before thee have apostles already been charged with falsehood: but they bore the charge and the wrong with constancy, till our help came to them; -for none can change the words of God...And the words of thy Lord are perfect in truth and in justice: none can change his words: He is the hearing, knowing (Q.6:34,115).*

*For them are good tidings in this life, and in the next! There is no change in the words of God! This is the great felicity (Q.10:64).*

*Will they say, 'He hath devised It?' SAY: If I have devised the Koran, then not one single thing shall ye ever obtain from God! He best knoweth what ye utter in its regard! Witness enough is He between me and you! And He is the Gracious, the Merciful. SAY: I am no apostle of new doctrines: neither know I what will be done with me or you. Only what is revealed to me do I follow, and I am only charged to warn openly (Q.46:8-9).*

Yet, Muhammad introduced himself as the authoritative figure, able to abrogate Allah's verses in the Qur'an. He states in some areas of the Qur'an that his verses are better than those of Allah and therefore he substitutes his own "better" or "similar" verses;[77]

> *Whatever verses we cancel, or cause thee to forget, we bring a better or its like. Knowest thou not that God hath power over all things?... Would ye ask your apostle what of old was asked of Moses? But he who exchangeth faith for unbelief, has already erred from the even way (Q.2:106,108).*

> *And when we change one (sign) verse for another, and God knoweth best what He revealeth, they say, 'Thou art only a fabricator.' Nay! But most of them have no knowledge (Q.16:101).*

> *Will they say, He hath forged it? Nay, it is the truth from the Lord that thou mayest warn a people to whom no warner has come before thee, that haply they may be guided (Q.32:3).*

This substitution caused his contemporaries to accuse him of slandering God. People mainly accused him because of his own claim that the Qur'an could not be inspired or changed by anyone.

---

[77] To find the verses that Muhammad substituted with Allah's verses, read Gerhard Nehls, *Christians Ask Muslims,* PP. 11-15.

Among Muhammad's associates, there were some enslaved scholars from different nations, who were released from slavery by Muhammad and joined his movement. Muhammad was not familiar with the languages of other religions and so he had no easy access to them. The other religions were open to him only through his foreign associates. After Muhammad's immigration to Medina, the recitation of the values of other beliefs by him as his own became widely obvious to people, resulting in their rejection of him. The following quar'anic verse proves that a large number of people in the Peninsula of Arabia knew of his heavy reliance on enslaved scholars from other religions and he had no choice but to publicly defend himself;

*We, also know that they say, 'Surely a certain person teacheth him (Muhammad).' But the tongue of him at whom they hint is foreign[78], while this Koran is in the plain Arabic (Q.16:103).*

It is because of this that there are parts of the Qur'an that strongly resemble different traditions and literature from other religions and beliefs. The Qur'an contains many themes that appear in the Old Testament, New Testament, Apocrypha, Talmud (Haggadah), and the Avesta - the book of

---

[78] The actual word for "foreign" in Arabic is "A'jami" that refers to the language of Salman Parsi, which is Farsi or Persian.

Zoroastrians.[79] One example - Jesus Christ as 'the Word and the Spirit of God' - is taken from the New Testament although it does not fit with the theology of Islam. Another example is the idea of the *bridge of sirat*[80] (Chinvat or Chinvad in Zoroastrianism), that finds its origin in Zoroastrian belief.[81]

For hundreds of years before the rise of Islam, the Jews brought about a remarkable change in the religious lives of the Arab people. Their customs and

---

[79] R. B. Smith, *Mohammed and Mohammedanism,* London, 1889, P.146. & J. Gilchrist, *The Textual History of the Qur'an and the Bible,* Reprinted by WEC International, 1987, PP.34-6. & H. J. Heydt, *A Comparison of World Religions,* Pennsylvania: Christian Literature Crusade, 1976, P.66. & R. Machatschke, P.1. & G. Nehle, P.100-101.

[80] Allah sets the *Bridge of Sirat* over hell. The pathway of the bridge is sharp like a sword or thin like a string of hair. Only Muslims that are more dedicated will be able to cross this bridge and enter paradise. Those who cannot cross the bridge are the condemned people. They will fall into the fiery lake of hell. According to Islamic traditions, Muhammad can turn this impossible situation into possibility for the condemned dead people if they call for Muhammad's intercession.

[81] Yasna1 (19:6), P.208 and Yasna2, P.201. The Vendidad (book2) translation by Hashem Razi, in Persian, 1997 (1376), P. 831. & Khordeh Avesta, edited by Rashid Shahmardan, Bombay-India: Published by P. P. Bharucha, Hon. Secy, The Iranian Zoroastrian Anjuman, 1929 (1308), P.177. Also see J. R. Hinnells, *Zoroastrianism and the Parsis, P.10,32.* & E. G. Parrinder, *A Book of World Religions,* P.115.

traditions were known to and practiced by many Arabs.[82] This may be one of the reasons for the Apostle Paul's journey to Arabia (Gal 1:17).

Scholars state that Muhammad himself was almost Judaized. It is in this way that the Qur'an owes a tremendous debt to the Hebrew writings and traditions. However the Qur'an is not drawn so much from the written but the oral Jewish law and traditions which grew around it.[83] It was because of Muhammad's illiteracy that he was not able to lean on the written scriptures of other religions but rather had to rely on the traditions or the word of mouth of his associates. His borrowing from other oral religious traditions may be a contributing factor in Islamic superstition, as oral tradition may be tainted by superstition.

A comparison between the Qur'an's material with other contemporary religious traditions and writings certainly proves that Muhammad has borrowed a lot of the Qur'an's materials from them.[84]

Muhammad was fully aware of the importance of Judaism in the peninsula of Arabia. For this reason he could not avoid it and leaned heavily upon it

---

[82] A. I. Katsh, *Judaism and the Koran,* New York: A. S. Barnes and Company, Inc., 1962, Indtroduction.
[83] R. B. Smith, P. 46.
[84] Ch. C. Torrey, *The Jewish Foundation of Islam,* New York: 1933, P. 61.

while also using both Christian[85] and Zoroastrian traditions for the advancement of his new structure.[86] He traced his own genealogy to Abraham through his son Ishmael, saying that - God could not omit the Arabs from the revelations with which He favored the Arab's cousins -the Jews and the Christians.

Muhammad believed that both the Torah and the New Testament had writings about him (Q.7: 157; 61:6). He considered himself the seal of all the Prophets;

> *Muhammad is not the father of any man among you, but he is the Apostle of God, and the seal of the prophets: and God knoweth all things* (Q.33: 40).

However, the Qur'an along with the Bible states that the prophetic line has come from the house of Isaac and Jacob, not Ishmael the forefather of Muhammad (Q.29:27).

He also considered Islam superior to all religions;

> *He it is who hath sent His Apostle with the Guidance and a religion of the truth, that He make it victorious over every other religion,*

---

[85] Colin Chapman, PP. 114-115.
[86] We know from the Qur'an that Muhammad's contemporaries accused him of being taught by someone (Q.16:103).

*albeit they who assign partners to God be averse from it* (Q.9: 33).

One reason for Muslims calling the Qur'an the highest and the greatest among the NT and OT is their belief that the Qur'an came down through one human instrument, whereas the Bible came down via many prophets. They believe too that the author of the Bible is God and the original manuscripts are in heaven. Muslims totally reject the authorship of the Books of God by any man. They believe that the Bible and the Qur'an came down as a verbal transmission from heaven and the prophets are only the bearers of the words of God.

Contrary to this, we are told in the Bible that God called, enabled and inspired many humans as instruments to reveal His will so that it could be related to others' thoughts and hearts and make sense to them. God's revelation must be inter-linked with human experience in order to make sense. The Bible says that the Word and the Spirit of God became flesh and was the body of Jesus Christ, the Son. The title "Son" means the Word and the Spirit of God came to share in the lives of humankind in order to make the difference between eternal life and death understandable and to make salvation holistic, applicable to mind, body, soul and spirit (Heb.2:14-17).

# SECTION FOUR:

# Misinformation By Muslim Evangelists

The causes of Muslim misinformation about Christianity are a product of political, economic and social factors at the time of the rise of Islam. Islam as a political religion legitimised political control over all aspects of life, in order to turn the diverse tribes of the Peninsula of Arabia into one Muslim community. To run their political course for reaching other nations, they chose a forceful one-way view with no right of free choice for other nations. Therefore, for the nations, the only choice was to accept Islam. Because of Islam's absolutist one-way approach, those who did not accept Islam were introduced to Muslims as those who were in error. Muslims could only conclude that there must have been some impediment to understanding amongst the nations who did not accept Muhammad as the seal of the prophets of God. The contemporary Christian communities also were not exempt from these types of thoughts and accusations when it came to evangelism. The result has been hatred between these two communities.

The best way to overcome this tragedy that has so harmed the relationship between Muslims and Christians right from the beginnings of Islam, is to study the words of the Qur'an and the Bible. These two books need to be compared by considering a great question. The question is 'How can humankind get rid of hatred of any kind, including religious hatred, and thereby unite with one another on the basis of eternal peace?'

This section touches the basis of several areas of misinformation by Muslim evangelists concerning Christianity.

## Measuring the Christian Message by Failure in Lifestyle

The failure of Christians when it came to following the standards of Christ drew a wrong picture of the Christian faith in the minds of Muslims. This in turn caused Muslims to accuse Christians of being corrupt and members of an incomplete religion. These accusations were empowered by continual propaganda. Muslims asserted that Christianity fell short of meeting the life needs of people and that it ought to be replaced with Islam.

Muslims were not aware of the central message of the Bible and of what Christ did on the Cross. What Muslims heard from Muhammad's mouth was taken as sufficient proof for rejecting the Christian faith. What they saw from the traditions and religious lives of those living in Christian society, they perceived as something portrayed in the pages of the Bible. Because of their lack of knowledge about the Bible, they were not able to distinguish the difference between carnal, contemporary Christian lives and the life led by the Spirit of the Bible. They assumed they were the same. Year after year Muslims without knowledge neglected and ignored the Bible more than ever. They adapted their faith and movement so that it took on a nature of bigotry causing a major rift between Muslims and Christians.

The accusations of Muslims against the Christian faith have remained out of touch with the words of Jesus Christ ever since the rise of Islam. Many times, we have heard fanatical Muslims on radio, TV, in taxis and in their newspapers accusing Christians of killing Muslims in the Crusades, in Bosnia, etc. Whilst concluding Christianity is to blame, they show ignorance of the words of Jesus Christ from whom Christianity originated who says, 'our struggle is not against flesh and blood but against the spiritual forces of evil' (Eph.6:12).

Muslims do not know that Jesus' philosophy is to love all humankind, no matter what their situation, and to hate Satan. Jesus sacrificed himself for all humanity in order to release them from the clutches of Satan. Muslims do not know that the love of Jesus Christ, the Son of the Almighty God, is for Christians, Muslims, Jews, the godly, the godless; in short, for the entire universe. For him no one nation is better than the other because all are from Adam and Eve, all have fallen short of the glory of God and therefore all are in need of salvation. Jesus has chosen love as the means for reconciling the nations to each other and to Himself.

Muslim evangelists didn't measure the intended quality of life for a Christian by studying the values of Jesus Christ. Instead, Muhammad and Muslim evangelists have been viewing the immoralities and temptations lived out by those bearing the name of 'Christian'. They have not discerned the work of the devil in the lives of these individuals and societies and have blamed their poor conduct on Christian values and teaching. They therefore present Christianity and the teachings of Christ as worthless and inferior to Islam;

*O believers! of a truth, many of the teachers and monks[87] do devour man's substance in vanity, and turn them from the Way of God (Islam). But to those who treasure up gold and silver and expend it not in the Way of God, announce tidings of a grievous torment (Q.9:34).*

## Incomplete Religions

Muslims hardly ever hear the Christian message, because they have been informed that Islam is the best, last and most complete religion after Judaism and Christianity, and Muhammad is the last, true prophet of all;

*Muhammad ... is the Apostle of God, and the seal of the prophets... (Q.33: 40).*

*He (God) it is who hath sent His Apostle with the Guidance and a religion of the truth, that He may make it victorious over every other*

---

[87] Christian monks.

*religion, albeit they who assign partners[88] to God be averse from it* (Q.9: 33).

*The true religion with God is Islam...* (Q.3:19).

Therefore, whatever the previous religions teach, they are incomplete in themselves.

## The Bible – Accurate or Altered?

The Qur'an states that Jesus and the prophets of the Old Testament foretold the coming of Muhammad;[89]

*Who shall follow the Apostle, the unlettered Prophet whom they shall find described with them in the Law and Evangel[90]... (Q.7:157).*

*And remember when Jesus the son of Mary said, 'O children of Israel! of a truth I am God's apostle to you to confirm the law which was given before me, and to announce*

---

[88] The Qur'an attributes the word 'partners' to pagans who call idols the children of God, and to Christians who call Jesus the Son of God and consider him on the same level as God. The word 'partner' or 'associate' is considered as offensive and demeaning.

[89] For further information read Ibn Hisham, *Sirat Raul Allah,* PP.203,204,206. & A. M. A. Shahrestani, *Tozih-almelal,* P.291 from book1.

[90] Or 'the Torah and the Gospel'.

*an apostle that shall come after me whose name shall be Ahmad!'*[91] *But when he (Ahmad) presented himself with clear proofs of his mission, they said, 'This is manifest sorcery!'* (Q.61:6).

These statements do not exist in the Bible. For this reason, Muslims explain that the Bible lacks the prophecies about Muhammad, because its followers altered its verses.

Muslims need to realize that there are more documentary evidences for the reliability of the Bible, than for any other book from the ancient world.[92] With the availability of these evidences it is impossible to build a case for where, when, how, and for what reason the Bible was changed. There is no time, whether during the time of Muhammad or before or after him, in which Muslims can prove that any alteration in the Bible occurred. The Qur'an itself confirms and defends the Bible, as it existed in the seventh century, as the word of God;

*...it* (the Qur'an) *be the truth confirmatory of their* (Christians and Jews) *own Scriptures...,...the confirmation of previous revelations,* (Q.2:91,97).

---

[91] Equated by Muslims with Muhammad.
[92] N.L. Geisler & A. Saleeh, PP.207-255. & North African Mission, *Reaching Muslims Today*, P.26.

*...believe in what* (the Qur'an) *we have sent down confirmatory of the Scripture in your* (Christians and Jews) *hands...* (Q.4:47).

*And if thou* (Muhammad) *art in doubt as to what* (the Qur'an) *we have sent down to thee, inquire at those* (Christians and Jews) *who have read the Scriptures before thee...*(Q.10:94; c.f. Q.3:3; 5:46-48; 29:46; 6:92; 41:43).

These verses of the Qur'an reflect Muhammad's high view of biblical authority. He confirms the authority of the Bible and therefore commands Muslims to profess belief in the same Bible that his contemporary Jews and Christians were holding. Therefore, the Qur'an itself takes away any reason for the Muslim rejection of the authenticity of the Bible.

In fact, Muhammad himself doubted the Qur'an, needing to lean towards the Bible and to judge accordingly (Q.10:94-5). Although the Bible was not translated into the Arabic language at the time of Muhammad, meaning he was unable to understand it, he still confirmed the authenticity of the current Bible possibly through the knowledgeable people who surrounded him. According to certain Qur'anic passages, he sometimes preferred to lean on the Bible rather than the Qur'an alone which was in his own language. He valued the Bible and only criticized those followers of the Bible and certain Christian groups who misinterpreted it or concealed the Scriptures from the people. He did not accuse them of corrupting the Bible; instead, he acknowledged the divine revelation of the Bible, the Bible that was read by contemporary Jews and Christians;

> *Desire ye then that for your sakes the Jews should believe? Yet a part of them heard the word of God, and then, after they had understood it, perverted it, and knew that they did so* (Q.2:75).

> *...the Book which Moses brought, a light and guidance to man, which ye set down on paper, publishing part, but concealing most* (Q.6:91; c.f. Q.2:146, 159, 174; 4: 46; 5:13-15, 41).

However, Muslim apologists, contrary to the Qur'anic passages, developed a baseless accusation against Christians and Jews accusing them of corrupting the Bible. They realized the existing inconsistencies between the Qur'an and the Bible, but were not able to compare them logically and theologically and discover the real reason for the disunity.

Diving into the depths of the world of reasoned thinking and research in Islamic societies has always been costly. Many who have done this have been excluded from their social rights and even sentenced to death. For this reason many dare not study the facts and the evidence in order to avoid mistreatment by Islamic authorities or even their own followers. They therefore prefer to follow in the traditional footsteps but in a different manner. For example, they accuse Christians and Jews of misinterpretation of the Bible both during and after Muhammad's time.

For Muslim scholars, the validity of the Bible is surprisingly not based on whether the book provides salvation or not; rather it is based on whether the book contains the name of Muhammad or not. How many Muslim scholars have shown any interest in discovering whether the Qur'an or the Bible best meets the immediate need of humankind for salvation? All they have done is to explain the difference between the Qur'an and the Bible according to the doctrine of corruption and alteration of the written text. Their goal is to discourage Muslims from reading the Bible even though the Qur'an gives that permission.

It is time for Muslim leaders and scholars to help their followers and readers to understand the real differences between these books by comparison of the qualities of the Qur'an and the Bible regarding salvation. This is more productive than concentrating on issues that have nothing to do with eternal destiny. What people need to discover is how they can be joined to their Creator immediately; no matter through which religion it can be gained. Wise leadership is one that bases its motives on people's real needs and leads them to achieve their needs through personal experience.

A Christian man who was from an Islamic background answered a lady's comment about the Bible having been altered. He said, "The Bible that you think has been changed, has changed the status of my life from the dominion of darkness to the kingdom of heaven". What really mattered for that person was that the words of the Bible have a saving power that saved his life, no matter what other people thought or said about it.

Curiously, Muslim scholars still give credence to some of what the Bible says. While on the one hand Muslim scholars disclaim the authenticity of the bible, on the other hand they are prepared to take its scriptures and interpret the verses to support their own claims about the prophetic ministry of Muhammad.[93]

The vital thing that makes the Bible different from the Qur'an is not the absence of Muhammad's name in the Bible, but the assurance of salvation that it contains. The Bible testifies to the salvation that God has provided through His Son, Jesus Christ. No such assurance of salvation is to be found in the Qur'an.

My initial interest in the Bible was not because of the name of Jesus Christ or the fact that He was called God's Son. Such ideas were as obstacles to me because of my irrational Islamic approach to the Bible. However, it was my certain need of salvation

---

[93] Read N.L. Geisler & A. Saleeh, PP.147-154.

that drew my attention to the pages of the Bible. For me to meet God and gain eternal life was the most important thing. This unavoidable need for eternal life led me to put everything else at a lower priority than my salvation. I therefore sought to approach the words of the Bible in its truest sense;

> *Your covenant with death will be annulled; your agreement with the grave will not stand* (Isa.28:18).

> *...my eyes have seen your salvation, which you have prepared in the sight of all people, a light for revelation to the Gentiles and for glory to your people Israel* (Luke2:30-32).

> *"God has come to help his people." This news about Jesus spread throughout Judea and the surrounding country* (Luke7:16-17).

> *"For God so loved the world that he gave his one and only Son, that whoever believes in him shall not perish but have eternal life* (John3:16).

> *I* (Jesus) *tell you the truth, whoever hears my word and believes him who sent me has eternal life and will not be condemned; he has crossed over from death to life* (John5:24).

My spiritual needs led me to test the words of the Bible against all the dimensions of my life.

Wonderfully my needs were met by the words of the Bible that acted as the power of God unto my salvation. Therefore, because of this awe inspiring experience my soul united with the life giving Spirit of the Bible who is called Jesus, the one who is God or the Son of God.

What is amazing about the Bible and has made it more reliable and trustworthy than any other book in the world, is the unity of its message on how God will come and carry on the work of salvation. Forty people wrote the whole Bible over about 1600 years. The passing of these many years could not erase the vital message of God from the pages of the Bible. Neither political conditions nor economic and social situations could create disharmony among the forty writers of the Bible over such a long period of time.

The message of the Bible is crystal-clear to everyone. It clearly says that no one except the Almighty God could save people from their sins. Therefore, everyone, including the prophets, relied on the saving act of the coming God (the Son), and taught others this Truth. Even the sins of the prophets were not a threat to the uniqueness of this message. The prophets and the great kings could not twist the promise of God in order to excuse their sins, because they had understood and believed the truth of the message. The only solution they found for their sins was to confess them regardless of the office they held (c.f., Ps.51; Isa.6:1-5). The book of Genesis in the Bible states that Christ, the Son, will come and destroy the work of Satan. This unchangeable promise of God became the faith of every writer of the Bible from the beginning to the end (Gen.3:15; 1John3:8). Therefore, by the Spirit of God all the writers of the Bible pointed people to the coming of the Son, Jesus Christ, who came with the full glory of God to save and unite people;

> .... *God was pleased to have all His fullness dwell in him* (Jesus), *and through him to reconcile to himself all things, whether things on earth or things in heaven, by making peace through his* (Jesus) *blood, shed on the cross* (Col. 1:19-20)

The revelation of God's full glory in Jesus Christ is the central message in the Bible that united the forty writers of the Bible over such a long period of time. Therefore the Bible remains unchanged and unaltered forever.

## The Qur'an – Complete Revelation from God?

Islam's own evidences – as they were mentioned earlier – prove that there are verses in the Qur'an which are not from Allah but merely from Muhammad and his companions. This contradicts the words of the Qur'an which presents the idea that if the Qur'an were from any other source than God, it would have been the source of contradictions;

*Can they not consider the Koran? Were it from any other than God, they would surely have found in it many contradictions (Q.4:82).*

However, we learn from Islamic traditions that the present Qur'an was rejected or accepted as incomplete by some of Muhammad's followers, including his successor and son-in-law, Ali.[94] This was mainly due to contradictions in this version of the Qur'an arising from a standardization attempt carried out by Uthman, the third successor after Muhammad's death. The vulnerability of the Qur'an, due to alteration of the text or replacement of certain texts, in turn, brought about divisions among Muslim leaders. This fueled disunity among

---

[94] Salim Ibn-Ghaisse (Death 90 H.G., 80 years after the death of Muhammad) writes in his book, 'It was the time of Uthman's caliphate that in a meeting Ali talked boldly and answered people's questions from morning to midday. He reminded the audience of what Muhammad said, 'Ali's relation to me is like Aaron's to Moses'. As part of the conversation, Ali confirmed that the Qur'an he collected was the most authentic and complete one. Parts of the present Qur'an were eaten by a sheep and many verses of the Suras (Chapters) 24, 33 and 49 were also missing. For further information read Salim Ibn-Ghaisse, *Asrar Aal Muhammad (The Mysteries of Muhammad's Descendants)*, Iran-Ghom: Translated by B. Alef, 1980? (1400 Hijri-Ghamari), PP.70-73,82-3.

them after Muhammad's death, even to the point of bitter rivalry or war.[95]

'At no time in Christian history has anyone attempted to standardize just one copy of the Bible as the true one while attempting to have all the others destroyed.'[96]   In contrast, Uthman ordered the destruction of all the other Qur'ans in circulation and presented the current text as the true standard. Islam's own theological and historical background proves that the present Qur'an can not be regarded as perfect and this is made very clear when one considers the many differences that existed among the various Qur'anic texts;[97]

- The Qur'an that has been standardized as correct is one which a *man* (not God), according to his *own choice* and not by revelation, decreed to be the true one.

- The theology of Islam speaks of one unchangeable heavenly text, whereas the

---

[95] While Muhammad was alive he realised that alterations of the Qur'an were causing divisions among his followers and he taught strongly in the Qur'an that any division would discredit the mission of Islam (Q.6:159).

[96] J. Gilchrist, *The Textual History of the Qur'an and the Bible,* Reprinted by WEC International, 1987, P.15.

[97] Read J. Gilchrist, *The Textual History of the Qur'an and the Bible,* PP.15-21. & Salim Ibn-Ghaisse, *Asrar Aal Muhammad,* PP.82-85.

followers of Muhammad had a variety of versions of the Qur'an.

- The evidence proves that the codex of Ibn Mas'ud was singled out by Muhammad as the best Qur'an available and this is not the basis for the present text (Sahih Muslim, Vol. 4, P.1312-3; Sahih al-Bukhari, Vol.5, PP.96-97).

- Qur'ans which differ not just in dialect but also textually certainly do not back up the argument that the Qur'an has never been changed. One example is that the present Qur'an borrowed the verse Q.33:23 from Khusaima-bin-Thabit al Ansari, a writer who was a contemporary of Muhammad (Sahih al-Bukahri, Vol.6, P.479).

- There is evidence that, to this day, verses and, indeed, whole passages are still omitted from the Qur'an (Ibn Ishaq, Sirat Rasulullah, P.684).

Therefore, no one can honestly claim that the Qur'an, in itself, has the authority of being God's eternal speech and his full revelation. 'If it is truly God's speech, it must be as eternal as He.'[98] If it were God's full revelation, there would be no

---

[98] K.Cragg, *The Call of the Minaret,* New York: Oxford University Press, 1956, P.54.

evidence of it being changed in any significant way. Clearly, this is not the case.

## Three Gods?

The Qur'an attributes to Christians' incorrect views about their belief in God. It says that Christians believe in three gods;

> *Infidels now are they who say, 'God is the Messiah, Son of Mary...They surely are infidels who say, 'God is the third of three:' for there is no God but one God: and if they refrain not from what they say, a grievous chastisement shall light on such of them as are infidels* (Q.5:72-73).

On one hand, the trinity that the Qur'an mentions is something quite different from the one that exists in the Bible and Christian faith. The Qur'an records that Christians worship **three gods**- *God, Mary,* and *Jesus*;

> *O ye people of the Book! ... say not, 'Three:'...* (Q.4:171).

> *And when God shall say - 'O Jesus, Son of Mary: hast thou said unto mankind - "Take me and my mother as two Gods, beside God?" '...* (Q.5:116].

This has led Muslims to believe that Christians are blasphemous and believe in various gods. Muslims, on the other hand, interpret the word 'Son' in a physical sense contrary to its real meaning in the Gospel. They say that God is spirit and therefore he could not have had a physical relationship with Mary producing a son like Jesus. Jesus is only a created man who was a prophet.

It is sad that for centuries Muslims have been rejecting Christians due to fallacious teaching. The Bible does not present Mary as a God, and Jesus' birth as the result of a physical relationship between God and Mary. In the Bible God is one, and has revealed Himself in three personalities, the Father, the Son and the Holy Spirit. With the coming of the Spirit upon the Virgin Mary, the Spirit became flesh (Jesus the Son) and revealed Himself fully. In the Bible, the understanding of the Trinity is something that leads the person to the only one and true God. This is the most gracious opportunity that the unique God has provided for all humankind, by becoming man, dwelling with us and relating Himself to us through His personalities. The Qur'an itself records this spiritual event (the coming of Jesus into the world) exactly as it is in the Bible;

> Remember when the angel said, "O Mary! Verily God announceth to thee the Word from Him: His name shall be, Messiah Jesus the son of Mary, illustrious in this world, and in the next, and one of those who have near access to God;... She said, 'How, O my

*Lord! shall I have a son, when man hath not touched me?' He said, 'Thus: God will create what He will; When He decreeth a thing, He only saith, "Be, and it is' (Q.3:45,47).*

Other texts from the Qur'an refer to Jesus being born as a man, but not the result of a physical relationship between God and Mary.

*... The Messiah, Jesus, son of Mary, is only an apostle of God, and his Word which he conveyed into Mary, and a Spirit proceeding from him...(Q.4.171).*

*...we (God) sent our spirit to her (Mary), and he (Jesus) took before her the form of a perfect man (Q.19:17).*

Unfortunately Muslims are not aware that these verses of the Qur'an mean that God became man (Jesus) and dwelt among His creatures.

The above verses carry the meaning that the *'Spirit of God'* and the *'Word of God'* became *Jesus*. God is Word and Spirit. The One and only God revealed himself in Jesus. It is the same as the Bible which proclaims that the Word 'God' or the Spirit 'God' became Jesus.

The following verses from the Bible support the Christian teaching of the Trinity.

*...the angel said to her, "Do not be afraid, Mary, you have found favor with God... "The Holy Spirit will come upon you, and the power of the Most High will overshadow you. So the holy one to be born will be called the Son of God (Luke1:30,35).*

*In the beginning was the Word, and the Word was with God, and the Word was God. He was with God in the beginning. Through him all things were made; without him nothing was made...The Word became flesh and made his dwelling among us. We have seen his glory, the glory of the One and only, who came from the Father, full of grace and truth (John1:1-3,14).*

These verses, whether from the Qur'an (see previous page) or from the Bible, speak of the Trinity. God sent His Spirit and the Spirit became Jesus (the Son). Introducing the Triune characteristics of God in the Bible has nothing to do with the matter of "three gods". In the Bible, the One and only God introduces Himself as the *Father*, the *Son* and the *Holy Spirit*. These three persons of the One God are one in nature and inseparable to one another and are united in God's eternal unity. Therefore, the three personalities of the One God cannot be treated as three separate gods.

Some Islamic commentators maintain that the spirit in the above Qur'anic verses (Q.4:171; 19:17) is not the Spirit of God, but the spirit of the Archangel.

This idea hardly fits with the theology of Islam. If the Qur'an does not accept that the Spirit of God became man, then it will also be hard to accept that the spirit of an angel, which is the angel himself, became man. According to the Qur'an, giving Jesus the title of God is 'the overstepping of Christians beyond their religious bounds' (Q.4:171). Similarly, giving Jesus the title of Archangel must also be seen in the same way.

We can understand from both the Bible and the Qur'an, that the Spirit that came upon Mary was from God and was God. The essence of such a belief reveals a great theological fact, which extends beyond the imagination of Muslims. The Bible says, *'The one who comes from above is above all; the one who is from the earth belongs to the earth, and speaks as one from the earth. The one who comes from heaven is above all. He testifies to what he has seen and heard'* (John 3:31-34). The Spirit that has come from above is revealed as a person who is above Adam and his descendants. Secondly, he is a Spirit that is from God (and was and will be with God), who became flesh and dwelt among humankind and who ascended back to heaven from where he came. The Spirit has always identified himself with God and Jesus. He is the spokesman of either Jesus or God, and this implies the interrelationship between Jesus and God. His prime reason for coming to earth is to be a man who reveals all that heaven has undertaken to save humankind. This teaching is not foreign to the verses of the Qur'an that talk about Jesus. The similarity arises from the fact that the Qur'an has borrowed the exact events from the Bible. In similar fashion to the Bible, the Qur'an also states that Jesus is the Word and Spirit of God who came down from heaven, became flesh, did the job for which he was sent and ascended back to heaven again. There is therefore an exact revelation of the Trinity when the Qur'an mentions the words, 'God, Spirit (or Word) and Jesus'.

The Trinity is not three gods. It is the three persons of the One God revealed as part of the plan of salvation to redeem us in all the dimensions of human life. God is one in His nature and essence, but his essence reveals his personalities to save sinful humankind according to his love, justice and holiness. God didn't have to reveal his persons. It was because of our needs that he stretched Himself towards us. God's work is not isolated from our needs in daily life. God is the loving God. What He desires is to have us back home. God is also holy and just. The triune personalities of God all work together simultaneously to open the eyes of people to accepting the saving acts of God.

When we invite God into our lives, and let his Spirit and Word and Love express his Oneness to us, only then will we be able to understand that the Trinity of the Bible is something that stands for One God not three. When Christians say that God is One, it is not simply a statement, but God's witness to the Truth through His Spirit. And his ministry can only be experienced by Christians through their faith in

Christ. It is the blessing of the three personalities of One God that has enabled Christians to meet God in Jesus Christ, the Son, and to call Him Emmanuel, which means, 'God with us' (Matt.1:23), not gods with us.

The idea of 'three gods' asserted by Muslim evangelists reflects their great misunderstanding of the Christian faith. This obstacle can be removed from the minds of Muslim evangelists only when they get the courage to read the words of the Bible in depth and so discover God's plan for salvation. They need to understand and to discover the central theme of the Bible, which is found through the authority of the Son's name, Jesus Christ.

## Teachers Equal with God?

The Qur'an accuses the Jews and Christians of claiming that their teachers and priests are equal to God;

> They (Jews and Christians) *take their teachers, and their monks, ... , as Lords beside God, though bidden to worship one God only. There is no God but He! Far from His glory be what they associate with Him* (Q.9:31).

This assertion is something very strange to the teaching of the Bible. The very convincing, simple and understandable message of the Bible is the uniqueness of God. Even every Jewish and Christian child knows that the whole story of creation, the stories of Noah, Abraham and the exodus from Egypt were the work of none other than the one and only living God.

There were ample worldly opportunities for the disciples of Jesus Christ, supported by their great miracles, to claim themselves as gods, but it was impossible for them, because they had understood that there was no god besides God. When the apostles Paul and Barnabas heard that people called them gods because of the miracle that Paul carried out, they both tore their clothes and rushed out into the crowd, shouting;

> *Men, why are you doing this? We too are only men, human like you. We are bringing you good news, telling you to turn from these worthless things to the living God* (Acts14:8-18).

It is very hard to believe that Jews called their teachers lords with the same status as God, when the main reason that Jews rejected Christians and started persecuting them was because they called Jesus God. There has never been a friendly acceptance of Christians by fundamentalist Jews because of Christianity's belief in the deity of Christ. Jews blamed Christians of claiming a man (Jesus) as equal to God. How then could they come to call their teachers lords?

The message of the Bible is based on the uniqueness of God from the beginning to the end. The Bible says that God is one and there is no one like Him.

Examples from the Old Testament:

*Who among the gods is like you, O LORD? Who is majestic in holiness, awesome in glory, working wonders* (Ex.15:11).

*My whole being will exclaim, "Who is like you, O LORD? You rescue the poor from those too strong for them, the poor and needy from those who rob them"* (Ps.35:10).

*Your righteousness reaches to the skies, O God, you who have done great things. Who, O God, is like you?* (Ps.71:19).

Examples from the New Testament:

*...God is one and there is no other but him* (Mark12:32).

*Is God the God of Jews only? Is he not the God of Gentiles too? Yes of Gentiles too, since there is only one God, who justified the circumcised by faith and uncircumcised throuyh that same faith* (Rom.3:30).

So, it is obvious that there is no substance to the assertion by Muslim evangelists that teachers are equal with God. There is no support for it in the teaching of Christianity and Judaism. Rather, Islam has distorted the truth to bring condemnation by its adherents against Christians and Jews.

# Teaching on Acceptance or Religious Discrimination

## So Much Sorrow for the Sons and Daughters of Adam and Eve

The misinformation spread by Muslim evangelists about Christians and Jews was extended to its highest level resulting in the total disqualification of these groups. Muslims are misled and told that they have to avoid any positive relationship with Christians and Jews, because they are from unclean nations. Christians and Jews can be regarded as clean only when they become Muslim. Therefore, any Muslim who touches a Christian or a Jew must be ceremonially washed.[99] This is the most upsetting of behaviours to be practiced by the fanatical children of Adam and Eve against their other brothers and sisters from the same root and substance. This must cause so much sorrow and embarrassment for Adam and Eve as parents, and must be an unbearable attitude in God's eyes, the one who has created all humankind from the same

---

[99] R. Khomeini, *Tozih Almasael*, Iran-Mashhad: Baresh Pub., 2000 (1379 Hijra), P.32,526. & A. Khamaneie, *Ajubatol-esteftaat* (in Dari Farsi), Tehran: Saghalain Pub., 1997 (1376 Hijra), P.92.

substance. This religious discrimination is also a dishonor to the world and cannot match with the message of peace among nations. Every person, who is familiar with the words of Christ, will understand that the theology of Islam has completely distanced itself from the loving Spirit of Christ whose task was to embrace everyone, Jews and Gentiles, equally (Eph. 1:9-10; Gal 3:28; 2 Cor. 3:17).

## In the Absence of the Gospel

Muslim evangelists often blame the Christian religion of being unable to discipline its followers for their immorality. In saying this they do not examine the Christian faith through the words of Jesus Christ, but through the behavior of those who claim to be Christians. Whenever they see immorality in any part of the Christian world, they see it as a defect of real Christian faith. They ignore and do not read about what the Gospel of Jesus Christ says about morality or immorality. This ignorance is because they think the Gospel is corrupted and hence they make no effort to discover the basis for Christian moral values in the Gospel. As a result, they have unfortunately judged the Christian faith in the absence of an understanding of the Gospel. They only look at the immorality of the Christian world, which is also alien to the faith of the Gospel of Jesus Christ, and use this as a basis for their criticism and rejection of the Christian faith. They believe that the immorality in the

Christian world results from the incompleteness of the Christian religion. This is a great theological mistake when someone criticizes a religion for the immoralities of its nominal followers without considering whether or not the religion itself is the cause of those immoralities. In a similar way, it would be wrong for someone to come and criticize Islam on the basis of the wrongdoing of Muslims, unless Islam presents itself to be the cause of that wrongdoing. For this reason, Muslims first need to discover whether the Gospel in the hands of Christians encourages the Christian world towards immorality or not. It is after this investigation that they will be able to realize the real cause of immorality in so-called Christian societies.

# SECTION FIVE:

# Ambiguities in the Teaching of Muhammad

# Politics or Theology?

Many Qur'anic verses and traditional statements bring forth the idea that Muhammad's decisions were subject to his own and his companions' unstable political trends rather than to an unchangeable God who is not capricious like man. He substituted Allah's verses in some parts of the Qur'an with that of his companions' and his own words in order to justify his actions. This instability meant that any idea accepted at one time could be rejected at another. Even the fundamental beliefs of his ministry would change according to the current situation. For example, while he was under pressure by the Meccan pagans in the first era of his ministry, he recited verses in praise of idols in order to win the favor of powerful pagan leaders and to gain momentum. Another example was when the prayer direction from Jerusalem to Mecca was completely changed. Before capturing Mecca, Muhammad recited the verses of Allah indicating that they had to pray toward Jerusalem, the dwelling place of the true God. However, after migration to Medina and falling into enmity with Christians and the Jews, he changed the prayer instruction of the Qur'an, not wishing to pray towards a city that belonged to his opponents, but rather towards Ka'bah, the pagan shrine in Mecca;

> *... The change is a difficulty, but not to those whom God has guided... we will have thee turn thy face to kebla...the sacred*

*Mosque[100]... Even though thou shouldest bring every kind of sign to those who have received the Scriptures (Jews), yet thy kebla[101] they will not adopt; nor shalt thou adopt their kebla;...(Q.2:143-145).*

These verses clearly state that the Muslims' previous Kebla was Jerusalem, which belonged to the Jews. They call upon Muhammad to no longer follow their direction. Instead, they tell him to turn his face toward Mecca, where he will find what satisfies his desires.

On the other hand, the Qur'an states that the house of worship (Ka'bah) in Mecca was made the holiest place of worship by God. God commanded both Abraham and his son Ishmael to build it for Muslims and to turn their face to it when they pray. After the completion of the Ka'bah the Qur'an states that Abraham prayed to God asking Him to make his posterity true Muslims and to raise a prophet among them to honour the rites and rituals of the religion of Abraham;

*The first temple that was founded for mankind, was that in Becca[102],... In it are evident signs, even the standing-place of Abraham: and he who entereth it is safe. And the pilgrimage to the temple, is a service*

---

[100] The house of worship in Mecca, called "ka'ba" which is equal to Temple.
[101] Kebla means "prayer direction".
[102] Place of crowding, i.e. Mecca.

> *due to God from those who are able to journey thither* (Q.3:96-97; also 2:125-129).

If these verses of the Qur'an were true words from God, why would Muhammad still have firstly selected Jerusalem rather than Mecca as the holy place of worship?

The initial rejection of Mecca and the acceptance of Jerusalem can only be understood in the light of two things. Firstly, Muhammad's friendship with contemporary Christian leaders who lived in the area and secondly, his attraction towards the widespread Jewish traditions rather than to Arabs and their traditions. Muhammad later gave up praying towards Jerusalem and chose Mecca as the prayer direction for Muslims as the Christians were no longer responding to his demands of them. He expected them to join his movement! When one considers the above, the only possible conclusion is that Muhammad's decisions were subject to his unstable political trends.

The Islamic tradition states Muhammad's *disinterest* as the definite reason for changing the prayer direction.[103] Traditions say that Muhammad's companions, who were from Medina, did not have a history of good relationship with the Jews even before the rise of Islam. The first non-

---

[103] Tabari, Muhammad-bin Jarir, *Tarikh-al-rosol val-molouk,* PP.941-2. & Ibn Hisham, *Sirat Rasul Allah,* P.536.

Jewish habitants of Medina who went to Mecca and accepted Muhammad's call were a group of six from the tribe of Khazraj who were the sworn enemies to the Jews in Medina. Khazrajites were pagan worshippers and were not befriended by the Jews. Jews continually threatened them by telling them about the coming of the future prophet (Messiah in the Biblical sense) who would end all blasphemy. Thinking that Muhammad was this Messiah, the Khazrajites made haste to gain the favor of Muhammad before the Jews. Therefore, they went to Mecca from Medina, made a mutual treaty with Muhammad and joined his movement. The treaty included vows made against the Jewish tribes in Medina. The Khazrajites vowed to welcome Muhammad into Medina and treat him as a member of their tribe. In return, Muhammad vowed to fight their enemies along with them and to make peace with anyone the Khazrajites called friends.

It was after this treaty that Muhammad's disenchantment with the Jews evolved. He legitimised war against non-Muslims and encouraged all Muslims to gather together in order to increase their strength so that a religious war could be enforced.[104] This of course angered the Jews because Muhammad was not a Jew but an Ishmaelite and therefore could not be the promised

---

[104] Tabari, Muhammad-bin Jarir, *Tarikh-al-rosol val-molouk*, PP.894-6,902-3,907-8. & Ibn Hisham, *Sirat Rasul Allah*, PP.426-29.

prophet. Secondly, Muhammad had made the treaty with the Khazrajites to get rid of the Jews. The Jews felt threatened and turned towards favoring the Meccans rather than Muhammad (Q.33:26). This fueled Muhammad's determination to make use of the above treaty. He launched various attacks on the Jews, resulting in their extermination and the rejection of the direction in which they prayed.

Another reason for the rejection of the Jews could have been related to their treatment of Salman Farsi, who was a slave placed in the hands of a Jew in Medina. As already mentioned, Salman was heading towards Mecca in order to visit Muhammad. Meccan caravan travelers sold him to a Jew. Salman had more than likely asked his Jewish master for permission to go and see Muhammad but was not permitted. However, Muhammad, after immigration to Medina released Salman, who later became a powerful Islamic figure.[105] Therefore, this event and similar ones might have contributed to Muhammad's growing anger towards the Jews.

Soon after, Muhammad started rejecting Christian beliefs. Christian communities therefore felt threatened and sent their leaders to Muhammad in order to hear his opinion face to face. Their intention was to solve the problem peacefully. However, Muhammad rejected their beliefs and

---

[105] Ibn Hisham, *Sirat Rasul Allah*, P.193.

placed before them two rigid options; to become Muslims or to pay tribute (jizya, a payment extorted to secure life).[106] It was after this, that he started to deny the sonship of Jesus Christ, His divinity and the Trinity. Before, he stated that Christians were above all others. He recited his so-called inspired friendly decrees to other religious groups giving them assurance that they needed not to fear and grieve;

> ... God said,...I will place those who follow thee (Jesus) above those who believe not, until the day of resurrection (Q.3:55).

> Verily, they who believe (Muslims), and they who follow the Jewish religion, and the Christians, and the Sabeites - whoever of these believeth in God and the last day, and doeth which is right, shall have their reward with their Lord: fear shall not come upon them, neither shall they be grieved (Q.2:62).

However, he later announced his most heartbreaking and shocking decree, saying;

> ...kill those who join other gods with God wherever ye shall find them: and seize them, besiege them, and lay wait for them with every kind of ambush: but if they shall convert, and observe prayer, and pay the

---

[106] Ibn Hisham, *Sirat Rasul Allah,* PP.188-9,491-516.

> *obligatory alms, then let them go their way,*
> *for God is gracious, Merciful* (Q.9:5).

All these prove that Muhammad's decisions stemmed from his fluctuating day-to-day political stance towards other nations and religious groups, rather than from a theological fact.

## Teaching on Forgiveness of Sin and Salvation

The misinformation Muslims have about Christian belief will be removed one hundred per cent when the ambiguity of Muhammad's ministry and teaching about sin and the forgiveness of sin is compared with the redemptive work of Jesus Christ.

Muhammad was ambiguous about his and his followers' future, and in one instance he gave shocking news to Muslims that they would first be taken to hell;

> *...neither know I* (Muhammad) *what will be done with me or you...* (Q.46:9 and c.f. Q.7:188).

> *Man* (Muslims and non-Muslims) *saith: 'What! after I am dead, shall I in the end be brought forth alive? Doth not man bear in mind that we made him at first, when he was nought? And I swear by the Lord, we will surely gather together them and the Satans:*

*then will we set them on their knees round Hell: Then will we take forth from each band those of them who have been stoutest in rebellion against the God of Mercy: Then shall we know right well to who its burning is most due: No one is there of you who shall not go down unto it −this is a settled decree with thy Lord- Then will we deliver those who had the fear of God (Muslims), and the wicked will we leave in it on their knees* (Q.19:66-72).

However, contrary to Muhammad's uncertainty, the Qur'an speaks of the certainty of Jesus Christ's ascension to heaven (paradise), a statement in line with the teachings of the Bible;

*He was taken up into heaven* (Lk.24:51).

*Remember when God said, 'O Jesus! verily I will cause thee to die, and will take thee up to myself and deliver thee from those who believe not* (Q.3:55).

*God took him up to Himself. And God is Mighty, Wise!* (Q.4:158).

Of some interest also is the Qur'an's belief that the followers of Christ (Christians) hold a higher spiritual position than those who do not believe;

*God said,...I will place those who follow thee* (Jesus) *above those who believe not, until the day of resurrection* (Q.3:55).

This Qur'anic verse is a clear reflection of the many verses in the New Testament which testify to Jesus' saving power;

*He* (God) *rescued us* (followers of the Son, Jesus Christ) *from the dominion of darkness and brought us into the kingdom of the Son he loves, in whom we have redemption, the forgiveness of sin* (Col.1: 13; also read Lk. 2:30-31; Jn. 5:24).

Muslims, therefore, need to realize Jesus Christ as the only one who truly rescued His followers from the dominion of hell. The Qur'an does not teach the same about Muhammad for Muslims. Why would a true prophet of God not be sure of his future state? This kind of uncertainty surely casts doubts on a religion claiming to be the best, last and most complete religion of all. If this is so, then why has man been moved from a position of assurance in Christ, to one of doubt in Muhammad? This isn't what you would expect if Muhammad was responding to the call of a caring and Mighty God. The purpose of God in sending prophets is to call back people to Himself. If a prophet is not sure of his future, how then will he be a good example to other people? How can a prophet, as yet non-saved, be a bearer of God's divine message of salvation? How can an uncertain man become the messenger of the certainty that he has not yet experienced himself? If God reveals His word to a person shouldn't he be sure of his destination? Is not God's message or mission all about creating assurance in the hearts of people? Why would someone submit himself to God without this assurance? Doesn't submission to God carry with it admission to heaven?[107]

A true prophet of God must be someone who is certain of his own salvation and becomes the very example of liberty amongst people. In biblical faith, not only the prophets but also every one who trusts in Christ the Son for deliverance from the bondage of sin, enjoys the certainty of salvation and freedom. They become the voice of salvation for every other person in the world. Those who enter into the covenant of righteousness and salvation with Jesus Christ through faith in Him, are preserved for eternity in heaven and the power of hell will not overcome them;

> *And I* (Jesus) *tell you that you are Peter, and on this rock I will build my church, and the*

---

[107] Tradition states; when the time of Muhammad's prophetic mission arrived, three angels came down to him, split his stomach, filled it with wisdom and assurance and removed all doubts from him (Tabari, Muhammad-bin Jarir, *Tarikh-al-rosol val-molouk,* PP.853-4 and cf. Q.74:1-4). This is quite opposite to the uncertainty Muhammad felt, according to the Qur'an (Q.46:9), years after his prophetic claim.

*gates of Hades* (Hell) *will not overcome it* (Matt.16:18).

*Blessed are the pure in heart, for they will see God* (Matt.5:8).

*And this is the testimony: God has given us eternal life, and this life is in his Son. He who has the Son has life; he who does not have the Son of God does not have life...you who believe in the name of the Son of God ... know that you have eternal life. This is the confidence we have in approaching God: that if we ask anything according to his will, he hears us. And if we know that he hears us - whatever we ask- we know that we have what we asked of him* (1Jn.5:11-15).

It is in this sense that a major difference exists between the Bible's and the Qur'an's beliefs. Those who have built their faith upon the Qur'an are uncertain about their salvation. But those who have built their faith upon the Bible have the seal of God's salvation within them and have tasted the freedom that they will have forever.

God is holy. He cannot have a relationship with any unsaved and unrighteous person. He also cannot demand the unsaved and unrighteous person to act righteously unless He Himself saves the person from the dominion of darkness and grants them righteousness. How can an unsaved person who is in the dominion of sin act righteously to please

God? How can we say a person is with God or God is with a person while that individual is still in the bondage of sin and Satan? Those who have not been brought back to mankind's original state of relationship with God as a result of salvation through the Son Jesus Christ are totally separated from God. They might have a desire for God and a yearning to be united to God, but it does not mean that they have been reconciled to God or have a relationship with Him.

## Teaching on the Search for Truth

When we call a religion the best and most complete of all, this means it has raised the certainty about a human being's salvation to its highest level in comparison to all other religions. It means that this religion has an attractive plan for reconciling humankind to God. But how can this be determined without searching amongst the various religions for truth? Do Muslims hold this view? If so they would be interested in knowing and understanding which is superior. They would want to find the religion that teaches genuine salvation, and would want to avoid the one that is hopeless and provides no certainty of salvation.

A true religion encourages its followers to a careful consideration of all things with the freedom to choose the best with a free will. God has not created us to accept or follow ideas and thoughts blindly despite his sovereignty over all things. Even He does not want us to follow Him blindly. Instead, He encourages understanding and acceptance that is based on weighing up the evidence, because knowledge and understanding are of His nature;

> ...the Lord is a God who knows, and by him deeds are weighed (1Sam.2: 3).

God has created and called us to be in His likeness - weighing up thoughts, words and deeds with open eyes, and making the best of all these things the basis of our own beliefs. The characteristics of belief in the Bible are having knowledge, understanding and choosing the best of all based on testing;

> But a prophet who presumes to speak in my (God) name anything I have not commanded him to say, or a prophet who speaks in the name of other gods, must be put to death. You may say to yourselves, "How can we know when a message has not been spoken by the LORD? If what a prophet proclaims in the name of the LORD does not take place or come true, that is a message the LORD has not spoken. That prophet has spoken presumptuously. Do not be afraid of him (Deu.18:20-22).

> "Come now, let us reason together," says the LORD (Isa.1:18).

*...people may see and know, may consider and understand,... "Present your case", says the LORD. "Set forth your arguments," says Jacob's King (Isa.41:20-21).*

*"Peace, peace," they say, when there is no peace (Jer.8:11b).*

*Jesus said, "...you will know the truth, and the truth will set you free" (John8:32).*

*...prophets should speak, and the others should weigh carefully what is said (1Cor.14:29).*

*Test everything. Hold on to the good (1Thess 5:21).*

*Dear friends, do not believe every spirit, but test the spirits to see whether they are from God, because many false prophets have gone out into the world. This is how you can recognize the Spirit of God (1John4:1-2).*

It is by research, knowledge and weighing up different words and beliefs that we will be able to find for ourselves the true Words of the true God, and then live them out as our own. However, if there is no knowledge of the beliefs and values of others and consequently no ability to compare them with one's own beliefs and values, then why should one call himself and his religion superior to others? If anyone knows the truth, that truth can set him or her free, but the truth cannot be found by blindly following or obeying the wrong guides who have never made a proper comparison.

There are verses in the Qur'an that encourage a search for greater knowledge about other beliefs in order to discover the best. Unfortunately, neither Muhammad nor his followers applied this in their lives;

> *For thy Lord is the most Beneficent, Who hath taught the use of pen; Hath taught Man that which he knoweth not* (Q.96:3-5).

> *On Earth are signs for men of firm belief, And also in your own selves: Will you not then behold them* (Q.51:20-21)?

> *And the blind and the seeing are not alike; neither darkness and light; nor the shade and hot wind* (Q.35:19).

This raises serious questions about the meaning of the word 'faith' in Islam. The word 'faith' in Islam implies the capability of every Muslim to understand the desires of God. In a Hadith (a tradition), Muhammad describes the faith as 'to acknowledge with the heart, to voice with the tongue, and to act with the limbs'.[108] Similar to what the Qur'an states, this hadith also recognizes

---

[108] W. C. Chittick, *Sufism*, USA: Oneworld Pub., 2000, P.6.

humanity's capacity for understanding the will of God.

All religions, in one way or another, call upon their followers to put their faith into action. What is crucial, however, is to use our mind to understand the religion in the context of life in the world. God's word must address itself to our mind so that we can use our intelligence to distinguish the right faith from the false. Therefore, knowledge is the inseparable part of faith. Knowledge discovers a place of confidence for faith to step into. Confidence, of course, is the result of a mind's search and is the positive result that stems from the experience of something that has been found. If someone decides to place confidence in God, it means that person has examined the word of God through the mind and heart and how it relates to all the dimensions of life, becoming confident to place complete trust in Him as the true God.

## God Is Unknowable?

For Muslims, God is beyond knowing, beyond consciousness, and even beyond being'[109] and he cannot be described by personalities. Therefore, 'in an effort to vindicate God's absolute unity, they stripped Him of His attributes'.[110] That is why 'the

---

[109] J. B. Taylor, P.14. & N.L. Geisler & A. Saleeh, PP.262-3.
[110] D. M. Lang, p.9.

heart of Islam is not to know God but to obey him. It is not to meditate on his essence but to submit to his will'.[111] As a result, 'God remains inscrutable and inaccessible to knowledge'[112]. This is the main reason why Muslims are not able to understand the Trinity of the One God. They have based their doctrine their Neo-Platonic[113] concept of oneness that views God as an absolute unity in which there is no multiplicity of characteristics at all and therefore unknowable.

Muhammad's own experience when he was receiving the first message of Islam from the Angel Gabriel conveys this same Islamic understanding of God. At the very beginning, the foundation of Islam was based on 'blind' obedience that did not require any knowledge about or understanding of the message. Gabriel forced him to simply recite words from his mouth that were incomprehensible to him. He stood against the force with all his strength. However, he could not stand the unbearable

---

[111] Ibid, P.137.

[112] K. Cragg, , P.55.

[113] Neo-Platonism developed from the philosophy of Plato's *theory of forms,* which says humankind's knowledge comes from recognising the essential form of a thing, rather than from observing its many incidental qualities. The Neo-Platonists carried the theory a step further, by saying that there is single highest form, *The One* that is incomprehensible. It is a mistake even to say that The One *'is',* because the one is beyond being (Neo-Platonism, The World Book Encyclopaedia).

pressure, gave up trying to resist and surrendered himself to the will of unknowable Allah. Allah armed Gabriel on the one hand with the Qur'an, and on the other with sufficient force to win the blind obedience of Muhammad. This became the process used for Islam's expansion ever since the rise of Islam as a state religion.

The way in which Muhammad received the Qur'an through an angel and not through Allah himself, unavoidably encourages Muslims to link their theology to the Neo-Platonic ideas about the invisibility and unknowability of God. How could an unknowable God, who did not expect Muhammad to comprehend him, expect Muslim scholars to comprehend him? So this gives Muslim scholars good reason to assert the unknowability of God, as God chose not to appear to Muhammad directly.

The unknowability of God in Islam opposes Muhammad's own claim concerning the superiority of Islam to the Jewish and Christian religions. In Judaism and Christianity God personally showed himself to the prophets and his followers. This is what the Qur'an also confirms (Q.4:164). Why would God choose direct revelation of Himself in a 'less important' religion but indirect revelation in Islam, a so-called superior and complete religion? Surely a complete religion necessitates a full and complete revelation? Indeed, a complete religion must remove all barriers and reveal God to His people, reconciling them to Him.

However, the 'unknowable' doctrine of Islam stands in opposition to the teaching of the Qur'an about God's relationship with humankind. This teaching includes the episode when God formed man from the dust by *'his hands'* and *'breathed'* into the dust and man became alive;

> *...Lord said to the angel, 'I am about to make man of clay, And when I have formed him and breathed my spirit into him, then worshipping fall down before him...whom my hands have made?* (Q.38:71,72,75).

The intimate relationship between God and Adam at the time of creation as described by the Qur'an does not fit with Muslims doctrine of the absolutist unknowable essence of God. How can we say that God breathed His spirit into Adam, dealing personally with him, and yet at the same time assert that Adam was a stranger to God? The above Qur'anic verses bring forth the meaning that Adam was not soulless dust anymore but someone who was carrying the witness about God. That was why the God of the Qur'an asked the angel to kneel down before Adam, who was able to introduce his creator and talk about His standards to the angel. The creation proves that God is a personal God who relates Himself to His creatures through His personalities.

The nature of the work of creation implies a tight connection between the essence of God, His works and His created man and woman. Men and women understood that they were created by God. God desired to create them. He translated His desire into action in order to have fellowship with them. He wanted to treasure them and to enjoy His mutual relationship with them. As a result, they were able to see who God was and the purpose of God in creation. There was not any kind of veil between God and the mind and heart of humankind at the time of creation. There was nothing causing a lack of understanding about God.

This changed when Adam sinned against God leading to the issue of a veil or separation between God and humankind. Such a separation became a serious threat for life on earth and after Adam sinned against God, God took the initiative to unveil the heart and mind of Adam. He helped him to tap into his God given understanding and capacity for remembering the beauty of God's presence with him before sin entered the world.

God created humankind with the ability to understand and He has continued His work of opening the heart and mind of humankind towards understanding. He has created humankind in such a way that they might understand Him. After Adam's fall, the work of God was always to unveil the mind and heart of each individual in order to enable each one to grasp and describe the fruitfulness and the beauty of His presence among them;

*O LORD, you are my God; I will exalt you and praise your name, for in perfect faithfulness you have done marvelous thing,...You have been a refuge for the poor, and refuge for the needy in his distress, a shelter from the storm and a shade from the heat... The sovereign LORD will wipe away the tears from all faces;... In that day they will say, "Surely this is our God; we trusted in him, and he saved us...let us rejoice and be glad in his salvation* (Isa.25:1,4,8,9).

The Son Jesus Christ came down from heaven to remove the veil, to free the world, and to return it to its first state of freedom. God in Christ revealed Himself to the world in order to open the minds and the hearts of the lost world and in this way to take them back to His kingdom (2Cor.3:12-18).

God is a revealing God, and He reveals Himself with all his personalities and characteristics, but only for those who are freed from their veils through their faith in the Son Jesus Christ.

It is impossible to have or to present the words of God without experiencing His personal presence and life changing works. The knowledge of God without the experience of God's presence is worth nothing. It is by experiencing the presence of God in our hearts, thoughts, words and deeds according to His will, words and works that the godly life makes sense. The experiencing of His presence, His words and works in religious language is called 'salvation'.

One reason that Islam offers no assurance of salvation is because it rejects the possibility of its followers experiencing God in the life on earth. That is why it has become so difficult for Muslims to comprehend the new life in Christianity. In Islam many attractive and elegant words were preserved carefully, sensitively, lovingly and sacrificially from generation to generation. They were made the influential and inseparable parts of culture, and in many cases the stronghold of one culture against other cultures, but still worthless for experiential salvation. The words of Islam can be memorized and kept in the mind, loved in the heart, but only as the words of a tradition or of a law. These people really fell in love with their religion and even put their lives on the line for their beliefs, yet their beliefs were unable to save them, in a spiritual sense. Their beliefs are not able to incarnate God in their hearts. They are unable therefore to leave a clear confession proclaiming that the job was completed, that they have reached their goals. They have no assurance that their bondage to Satan was abolished and that God is with and in them forever (Emmanuel).

If the doctrine of Islam, which testifies to the unknowability of God, was true, then the Garden of Eden would have allowed for no relationship between God and Adam and Eve. Accordingly, rebellion and sin would not make sense, as there would have been no intimate relationship between God and humankind that could be broken. Therefore, there was no need for humankind to repent and to long for fellowship with God. Likewise, there was no need for God to acknowledge humankind's confession. The Paradise that Islam looks forward to after death would not make any sense of an intimate relationship between God and humankind. It is therefore hardly attractive to the heart that seeks after God and asks for his protection. If the living spirit of a human being, given to that person by the living Spirit of God, cannot know the Creator, then nothing makes any sense; neither belief nor unbelief, nor rebellion, nor repentance, nor submission, nor godly living, nor judgment, nor paradise, nor acceptance, nor rejection, nor anything else, for the goal and joy of knowing God is unreachable. Therefore, any doctrinal interest in Islam fails to be convincing and furthermore, fails to meet the hunger and thirst of humankind for the Creator. 'How humankind takes shelter in God' is something that does not even make sense in Islamic doctrine.

It is instructive to understand that Muslims introduce themselves as the *Khalifatallah* (vice-regent i.e., God's representative). They fail to recognize that this isn't supported by their doctrine of the unknowability of God. God's reign cannot be manifested by Muslim rulers, when He is regarded as an inaccessible God by Islam's doctrine. If He is not accessible, He cannot sit upon any human throne and rule with appointed vice-regents.

Accordingly, none of the Islamic governments can call themselves the agents of Allah. Who can claim to be the ruler for God, when he is not able to sense the qualities of God's ruling Spirit?

If God is not understandable, then the Islamic mission of wanting to rule the world on behalf of Allah becomes invalid according to the doctrine of Islam. Even when Muhammad presents himself as the prophet of God, this does not fit with the Islamic doctrine that no one can submit to God (a complete contradiction to the meaning of Islam) and walk closely in relationship with Him. Furthermore, the Qur'an, which calls itself a guide for humankind to know God, cannot make sense. For example, the Qur'an introduces God as the compassionate and merciful God at the beginning of all its chapters. If God is unknowable, then what does compassionate or merciful mean? What does it mean, in the following Qur'anic verses, when it speaks of 'understanding'? Islamic scholars need to acknowledge this inconsistency.

> *An Arabic Koran have we sent it down, that ye might understand it (Q.12:2).*

> *We have made it an Arabic Koran that ye may understand. (Q.43:3).*

> *We have created man from the union of the sexes that we might prove him; and hearing, seeing, have we made him (Q.76:2).*

Paul, the apostle of Christ, has written eye opening words on how one person can understand God;

> *Who among men knows the thoughts of a man except the man's spirit within him? In the same way no one knows the thoughts of God except the Spirit of God. We have not received the spirit of the world but the Spirit who is from God, that we may understand what God has freely given us. This is what we speak, not in words taught us by human wisdom but in words taught by the Spirit, expressing spiritual truths in spiritual words. The man without the Spirit does not accept the things that come from the Spirit of God,... , and he cannot understand them, because they are spiritually discerned ... who has known the mind of the Lord that he may instruct him? But we have the mind of Christ* (1Cor.2:11-16).

## The Son of God?

The verses of the Qur'an about the sonship and deity of Christ contradict each other. The reason for this contradiction is that the Qur'an firstly has borrowed from Christian traditions and Scriptures out of context, and secondly, it has borrowed from other sources and arranged all these verses in such a way as to be very different from the Bible. However, it is obvious that the logic of the Qur'an's own verses does not reject the divinity of Jesus Christ. If

Muslim scholars and evangelists would carefully consider and analyze the relevant Qur'anic verses theologically, they would not be able to deny the divinity of Jesus Christ.

## God Had No Spouse

The Qur'an recounts the Christian doctrine that Jesus is the *Word* and the *Spirit* of God. It teaches that his birth was the result of the coming of the Word and Spirit of God upon the Virgin Mary, not as the result of a sexual relationship;

> *...when angel said, 'O Mary! Verily God announceth to thee the Word from Him: His name shall be, Messiah Jesus ... She said, 'How, o my Lord! shall I have a son, when man has not touched me?' He said, 'Thus: God will create what He will;...* (Q.3:45,47).

> *... The Messiah, Jesus, son of Mary, is only an apostle of God, and his Word which he conveyed into Mary, and a Spirit proceeding from him...*(Q.4.171b).

> *...we* (God) *sent our spirit to her* (Mary), *and he* (Jesus) *took before her the form of a perfect man* (Q.19:17).

> *And her who kept her maidenhood, and into whom we breathed of our spirit, and make*

*her and her son a sign to all creatures* (Q.21:91).

These verses of the Qur'an appear to be more closely related to the Bible based beliefs of Christians regarding Jesus' conception than to the many fanciful Islamic notions that have been floating around in the thoughts of Muslim evangelists throughout Islam's history. However, at the same time, the Qur'an accuses Christians of claiming that God had sexual relations with Mary in order to give birth to Jesus;

*... Far be from His glory that He should have a son* (Q.4:171c).

*Sole maker of the Heavens and of the Earth! How, when He hath no consort* (spouse), *should He have a son?...*(Q.6:101).

*SAY: He is God alone: God the eternal! He begetteth not, and He is not begotten; And there is no like unto Him* (Q.112:1-4).

The concept of Mary being God's spouse as referred to here by the Qur'an is totally foreign to the pages of the Bible. The Bible clearly states that to be called the sons or daughters of God carries solely spiritual meaning;

*Yet to all who received him, to those who believed in his name, he gave the right to become children of God – children born not of natural descent, nor of human decision or a husband's will, but born of God* (John 1:13).

*For you have been born again, not of perishable seed, but of imperishable, through the living and enduring word of God. For, "All men are like grass, and all their glory is like the flowers of the field; the grass withers and the flowers fall, but the word of the Lord stands forever." (1Pet.1:23-25).*

*Flesh gives birth to flesh, but the Spirit gives birth to spirit* (John 3:6).

Although the previous Qur'anic verses suggest God would never have a son, the following verse of the Qur'an carries the meaning that God can have a son if he desires;

*Had God desired to have had a son, he had surely chosen what he pleased out of his own creation. But praise be to Him! He is God, the One, the Almighty* (Q.39:4).

The concept in the above verse is conditional; 'If God desired to have had a son, he had...'. This means that according to the Qur'an, it is not impossible for God to have a son. Although the possibility of God 'having a son' threatens the teaching about the unknowable and unreachable God of the Qur'an, the Qur'an does not rule out the possibility of God having a son! This contradicts the

Qur'an's own stand in cursing Jews and Christians for attributing fatherhood to God;

> *The Jews say, 'Ezra (Ozair) is a son of God'; and the Christians say, 'The Messiah is a son of God.' Such the sayings in their mouths! They resemble the saying of the Infidels of old! God do battle with them! How are they misguided* (Q.9:30).

## The Son Incarnate!

The phrases the 'Spirit of God' and the 'Word of God' in the Qur'an (Q.4.171b; Q.19:17) carries the same meaning as 'God the Spirit' and 'God the Word'. When the Qur'an says that Jesus was born by the coming of the Spirit and the Word of God, it means, that Jesus was born by the coming of 'God the Spirit and Word' upon the Virgin Mary. In other words, God became man. This was the belief of the prophets of the Bible who foretold the revelation of God through Jesus Christ many hundreds of years before Islam and Christianity. They stated that the Almighty God would dwell among humankind by way of a Virgin. Isaiah, the eight century BC prophet says;

> *Therefore the Lord himself will give you a sign: The virgin will be with child and will give birth to a son, and will call him Emmanuel* (which means, "God with us") (Isa.7:14).

*For to us a child is born, to us a son is given, and the government will be on his shoulders. And he will be called Wonderful Counselor, Mighty God, Everlasting Father, Prince of Peace. Of the increase of his government and peace there will be no end. He will reign on David's throne and over his kingdom, establishing and upholding it with justice and righteousness from that time on and forever* (Isa.9:6-7).

The New Testament says that these prophecies were fulfilled when the Word and the Spirit of God appeared in the flesh of Jesus Christ with the fullness of His power, glory and grace;

*All this took place to fulfill what the Lord had said through the prophet: The virgin will be with child and will give birth to a son, and they will call him Emmanuel* (Matt.1:22-23).

*In the beginning was the Word, and the Word was with God, and the Word was God. He was with God in the beginning. Through him all things were made; without him nothing was made....The word became flesh and made his dwelling among us. We have seen his glory, the glory of the One and only, who came from the Father, full of grace and truth* (Jn.1:1-3,14).

Tabari, the notable ancient Islamic commentator and historian, narrated the visit of Mary, the mother of Christ, to Elizabeth, the mother of John the Baptist (Yahya), as following, which confirms the divinity of Christ. Mary asked Elizabeth, 'do you know that I am pregnant?'. Elizabeth answered, 'the one that is in my womb bowed down to the one in your womb, this is the confirmation of the Word of God'.[114] John who was not the word of God bowed down to the divine Word of God, Jesus.

## Spirit and Substance

The Qur'an also believes that spirit can become flesh;

> *When they* (angels) *went in unto him* (Abraham) *and said, 'Peace!'*...(Q.51:25 also 11:60; 15:52).

We learn from the Islamic tradition that the angel Gabriel appeared to Muhammad in various occasions as a man.[115]

The Qur'an again quotes the biblical narration that God showed Himself as fire (substance) to Moses;

---

[114] Tabari, Muhammad-bin Jarir, *Tarikh-al-rosol val-molouk,* P.518.

[115] Tabari, Muhammad-bin Jarir, *Tarikh-al-rosol val-molouk,* PP.510,849,1082-3. & Ibn Hisham, *Sirat Rasul Allah,* PP.212-13. & A. M. A. Shahrestani, *Tozih-almelal,* P.62.

*Hath the history of Moses reached thee? When he saw a fire, ... he came to it, he was called to, 'O Moses! Verily, I am thy Lord:... I am God: there is no God but me:...* (Q.20:9,11,12,14; also 28:29-30).

The Almighty God became a fire (a substance) and it did not seem blasphemous to the Qur'an. How then does it become blasphemous to the Qur'an when the Bible announces that God became flesh (substance)?

The word 'man' ('nass' in Arabic) is highly valued in Islamic doctrine. When the word 'Allah' is replaced by the word 'man', the meaning of many verses in the Qur'an is no different. Would it not be more acceptable for Muslims when God dwells in man than if he were to dwell in any other substance? Does the kind of substance God chooses to dwell in make a difference for the Qur'an? If it does not, then why does it blame Christians for claiming that God became man? And if it does make a difference, then why is it not more acceptable for Muslims when God chooses to dwell in the best of His creatures, man?[116] Isn't it man who is called to live under the rule of God? Isn't it man that is more precious to God than anything else? How can the Qur'an believe in the incarnation of Satan (who became a snake drawing people towards many kinds

---

[116] According to Muslims' conviction, man is God's vice-regent or khalifa in Arabic (Q.2:30).

of curses), and yet not believe in the incarnation of God (who became a man to draw humankind to heaven)? Is God an aloof, indifferent, merciless being when it comes to saving humankind, compared to Satan who is present in every affair of humankind and tries to destroy them?

## The Son the Creator

The Qur'an also unexpectedly attributes to Jesus the work of creation when it describes the life giving power of Jesus to create a bird in the same manner and sequence that both the Qur'an and the Bible attribute to God;

> ...Out of clay will I (Jesus) make for you, as it were, the figure of a bird: and I will breathe into it, and it shall become, by God's leave, a bird (Q.3:49; cf. Q.5:110).

The breath that Jesus breathed into the clay bird had the same power and characteristics as the breath of God in creation. If Jesus is not divine, how can His breath act in the same way as does the divine breath? Did this breath come out from inside of Jesus? Was that because God had made His dwelling in Jesus? Doesn't the breath of creation belong only to God? Did that bird really join the world of living creatures, or was it only magic? The

Qur'an says, it became a living bird.[117]  A bird that could become a testimony to the life giving breath that came out of Jesus.  Because of these verses and many others, the fact that the Qur'an denies the divinity of Jesus is something that brings the consistency of the Qur'an's theology into question.

## Once in Harmony with the Bible!

The start of Muhammad's life work was closely related to the Christian community.  His protests against idol worshipers, who called the idols the children of Allah, stems back to the advice of his Christian relatives and friends who taught him that the deity and sonship of Christ was the truth, not idols;

> *Do not make idols or set up an image or a sacred stone for yourselves, and do not place a carved stone in your land to bow down before it.  I am the LORD your God* (Lev.26:1).

> *The acts of the sinful nature are obvious: ... idolatry and...* (Gal.5:19).

---

[117] Tabari states in his, *'Commentary on the Qur'an'* (P.983) the bird that Jesus created was a 'bat' and flies at night..

> *But about the Son he* (God) *says, "Your throne, O God, will last forever and ever,...* (Heb.1:8).

Muhammad might not have understood the authenticity of the divinity and the sonship of Christ as the Bible describes it. However, he did not criticize or reject the idea in the first years of his friendly relationship with the churches. He was happy spending time with Christians and tried to prove that he was a friend, by adapting himself to their way of life. Otherwise, the church leaders in Mecca and Syria would not have been interested in supporting him. His respect towards Jesus as "Messiah (Christ), Word and Spirit of God" was proof of his eagerness in his early years of ministry, to place himself in line with the Bible's prophets who all willingly bowed to the coming God, as " Messiah and the Son of God" (Isa.7:14; 9:6-7; Matt.16:16; John1:1-3,14; cf. Q.4:171).

The titles "Messiah" and "the Word and the Spirit of God"[118] in the Bible are all attributed to Jesus because of His pre-eminent and superior characteristics among all creatures. It is not comprehensible that Muhammad was once in harmony with the Bible, with the prophets of the Bible and with influential Christian leaders, but at the same time denied the deity and sonship of Jesus

---

[118] For further information read, J. Gilchrist, *The Title of Jesus in the Qur'an and the Bible,* England: Roodepoort Mission Press, 1986.

Christ. He was with those Christians who believed in Jesus as "God, the Word and the Spirit of God, the Messiah and the Son of God". There is no evidence of Muhammad denying the above in his early ministry.

In addition to the above, the Biblical and Talmudic backgrounds of the Qur'an[119] are also proof of Muhammad's willingness to follow the faith of the Christian leaders with whom he was in close contact. Even if, in his later ministry he fell into enmity with Christians and Jews, he still could not erase the biblical flavour of his message that was there from the beginning. We see that he overwhelmingly tried to keep his message related to the Bible. Even in his exaltation, he still related himself to the Jews. He exalted himself above the Jewish prophets when he introduced himself as the seal of all the prophets descended from the Jews;

> ...the unlettered Prophet whom they (Jews) shall find described with them in the Law and Evangel...(Q.7:157; cf. Q.61:6).

> Muhammad is...the seal of the prophets (Q.33:40).

All the evidences show that from the beginning, Muhammad was in harmony with the Christian leaders and consequently, in favor of the deity and

---

[119] A. I. Katsh, *Judaism and the Koran,* New York: A. S. Barnes and Company, Inc., 1962, all pages.

sonship of Christ. However, this did not remain so. The changing characteristics of his political faith caused him to lose his Christian environment after his flee from Mecca to Medina. The Islamic tradition clearly proves that in Medina, in his confrontation with the Christian leaders, he totally denied the sonship and the deity of Christ.[120] He had gained great power from his new movement in Medina. No longer was he known as just a prophet anymore, as he was in Mecca, but greater than all and the seal of all. The religion he had created was also called superior to all other religions. Therefore, he could not call Jesus the Son of God anymore and he had to deal with all the Bible's teaching that were contrary to what he was asserting.

## Supreme Characteristics of the Son

The Son Jesus Christ, the Bible says, is God, greater than the angels and the prophets:

- The Son is alive from eternity to eternity and He is the exact representation of God's being and over all creation (Jn.1:1-3,14,18; 17:5; Heb.1:3; Col.1:15; Rev.11:15).

- The Son proves His equality with God (the Father) by the unique words and works He speaks and accomplishes (Matt.5:43-48; Jn.5:21-30; 11:38-39, 43-44).

---

[120] Ibn Hisham, *Sirat Rasul Allah,* PP.509-12.

Whatever God does the Son does also (Jn.5:19).

- The Son is greater than every prophet, greater than Abraham, Jacob, Moses, David, Solomon, Jonah, John the Baptist (Jn.8:53,56-58; 4:12-14; 5:46; Heb.3:5-6; Matt.22:43; Lk.11:31-32; Jn.1:29-30).

- The Son is 'love' and therefore, is for all humankind (1Jn.4:7; Jn.3:16).

- The Son became the unchangeable standard and eternal glory for Moses who, for the sake of the Son Jesus Christ as one of greater value, chose to be mistreated rather than to enjoy the pleasure of the kingdom of Egypt (Heb.11:24-26; Matt.17:3).

- The Son became the climax of all the prophecies in the Bible (Acts10:43).

- The Son is from heaven whereas all other prophets are from the dust of the earth (Jn.3:13; 6:38,42,62; 8:23; 16:28; 1Cor.15:47 ;cf. Q.19:17).

- The Son came down from heaven to take the lost back to his/her original state. This is what the prophets and the law could not do (Acts4:12; Gal.2:16).

- The Son, contrary to the prophets, is called the Word and the Spirit of God (Jn.1:1-3; Lk.1:35; cf. Q.4:171).

- The Son is *the way Himself* to heaven (Jn.14:6) whereas the prophets are only indicators to the way.

- The Son has power to lay down his life for many and take it again (Jn.10:18). Adam satisfied his sinful nature and in this way spiritual death came to all humankind, but Jesus satisfied the nature of God, laid down his life for all humankind and once again brought life to humankind (Rom.5:15-21).

- The Son appeared to destroy the devil's work and to bridge the gap between God and humankind (1Jn.3:8; Col.1:20; Matt.4:1-11) whereas no one prophet was able to do so.

- The Son has victory over sin, death and Satan (Heb.2:14).

- The Son can bring the dead bodies to life (Jn.11:43-44; cf.Q.5:110).

- The Son is greater than the angels and all angels worship him (Heb.1:4,6).

- The Son is alive and in heaven and rules over his people from heaven (Col.1:18).

- The Son provided the opportunity for humankind to have access to eternal life, which Adam deprived them of (Gen.3:24; Rev.22:14).

- The Son is the eternal source of salvation for all who believe in and follow him (Lk.2:31; 1Jn.1:7-9). He breaks the power of sin in everyone's life from the moment one believes in him, thus being assured of his/her salvation (Lk.7:48-49; Jn.5:24; 1Jn.5:13).

- The Son's message cannot be under the influence of the fluctuating 'Yes' and 'No' of worldly politics. Instead, His 'Yes' was always 'Yes' and His 'No' was always 'No' (Matt.5:37; 2Cor.1:18-22).

- The Son did not come to be served, but to serve, and to give his life as a ransom for many (Matt.20:28).

- The Son is interested in relationship with humankind in order to save them. He knows that everybody's heart cries for freedom. He, therefore, does not exclude anyone from His plan of salvation (Jn.3:16-17; Rom.3:23-26).

- The Son is the light of the *world* (Jn.8:12; cf. Q.3:3-4; 19:21).

- The Son knows the future (Lk.18:31-32).

- The Son will come again with glory to judge the world (1Thes.4:16; Matt.16:27; Jn.5:28-29; cf.Q.43:61).

- The Son has come and given us understanding that we may know the true God (2John5:20).

The above qualities are supremely above the characteristics of all humankind. They are heavenly qualities which supersede all earthly qualities. They are those qualities that only the Heavenly Ruler and King can possess. One must be God to have these qualities. These qualities do not fit with Muhammad's hypothesis in which he, as a man, tries to provide a purely 'of this world' explanation for Jesus Christ. These qualities are heavenly characteristics that can only be revealed and described by the Spirit of God. Humankind can understand it only when they open their ears to hear the words of the Holy Spirit. As Jesus described to His students, the meaning of the term 'the Son' cannot be revealed by man but only by His Father in heaven;

> ..."Who do you say I (Jesus) am?" Simon Peter answered, "You are Christ, the Son of the living God." Jesus replied, "Blessed are

*you Simon son of Jonah, for this was not revealed to you by man, but by my Father in heaven"* (Matt.16:15-17).

On the other hand, we can see these qualities are far beyond the objectives of Muhammad's ministry. They are the qualities of a sacrificial ministry that lays down divine life so all may come to realize love as being the most fundamental tool in unifying the nations of the world in One God;

*For God so loved the world that he gave his one and only Son, that whoever believes in him shall not perish but have eternal life* (John3:16).

These qualities were beyond Muhammad's power and he was not to show them in his ministry. For the success of his political movement, Muhammad, therefore, had no choice but to reject the sonship of Jesus Christ, and to introduce him as somebody lesser than he was. The sonship of Christ did not go with the greatness of his worldly political power. Therefore, he had to reduce Jesus Christ and introduce himself as someone greater than Jesus.

## The Son Reconciles People to God

The Son, for Christians and for Jews (the coming Messiah) is greater than anyone on the earth, including Muhammad. But in the Qur'an the Son is not given this status. In the Bible, the Son is from heaven and therefore can reconcile humankind to God, by rescuing us from the dominion of Satan and taking us to his heavenly kingdom;

> *For he (God) has rescued us from the dominion of darkness and brought us into the kingdom of the Son he loves, in whom we have redemption, the forgiveness of sins... For God was pleased to have all his fullness dwell in him, and through him to reconcile to himself all things, whether things on earth or things in heaven, by making peace through his blood, shed on the cross (Col.1:13,19-20).*

In other words, the Son takes people, whom Satan has separated from God, back to Him. There is no one except the Son Jesus Christ who can take people back to their original state. That is why Jesus said;

> *" I am the way and the truth and the life. No one comes to the Father except through me (John14:6).*

This truth is not taught in the Qur'an. So the actual difference between the Qur'an and the Bible is nothing other than the two quite different positions and roles attributed to Jesus Christ. In other words, in the Bible Jesus Christ holds a position as the supreme life-saver from heaven and in this way makes the Bible different to the Qur'an.

# Teaching Concerning Prophets

Contrary to Muhammad, the prophets of the Bible gave up their worldly fame to take shelter in the eternal glory of the coming Son. Moses sacrificed his political fame for faith in the coming promise. He resigned from the kingdom of Egypt just for the sake of the Son Jesus Christ, the eternal Redeemer (Heb.11:26).

Muhammad also, like all the prophets of the Bible, had a choice in front of him. He had to choose between *the Son Jesus Christ* (he accepted Jesus Christ as the Son of God early on in Mecca) *or the new political power, fame and pleasure* he had established in the world (in Medina for Muhammad). The Son of the Bible, who came to establish the eternal kingdom among the nations of the world, was left outside the heart of Islam. Instead, He was introduced as the one who tried his best to establish an earthly kingdom, but failed to do so. Muhammad, as the seal of the prophets, took over the task of completing an earthly kingdom and launched the march from Madina.

The growing Islamic belief system was going along a path that was not in line with the biblical path. Those who adhere to biblical teaching have the right to weigh the authenticity of the words they hear from any who claim to be a prophet. God said to Moses;

*If anyone does not listen to my words that the prophet speaks in my name, I myself will call him to account. But a prophet who presumes to speak in my name anything I have not commanded him to say, or a prophet who speaks in the name of other gods, must be put to death* (Deut.18:19-20).

In biblical faith, it is not the people who do not listen to the messages of God that must be put to death immediately. Rather, the one who calls himself a prophet and misleads people to accept his words as God's words must be put to death. Furthermore, God speaks through Moses to the people;

*You may say to yourselves, "How can we know when a message has not been spoken by the LORD?" If what a prophet proclaims in the name of the LORD does not take place or come true that is a message the LORD has not spoken. That prophet has spoken presumptuously. Do not be afraid of him* (Deut.18:21-22).

If these words are compared with what the Qur'an said (Q.4:150-152), it becomes clear that the two paths are going in opposite directions:

| *Biblical Path* | *Qur'anic Path* |
| --- | --- |
| - people have choice | - people have no choice |

| | |
|---|---|
| - people are not slaughtered because of their different faith | - people are slaughtered because of their different faith |
| - people have right to test whatever they hear | - people have no right to test whatever they hear |
| - people have right to enquire about the prophet's words and deeds | - people have no right to question the prophet at all |
| - prophet is accountable to individuals for his words and deeds, because every individual is called to look after the society both spiritually and physically | - prophet is not accountable to the society because the ultimate authority is in his hands. Individuals must obey him. |
| - people worship God and know him | - people worship God without knowing him |

In the Bible even the prophets humble themselves and say that there is not even one person on the earth who can be relied on as a standard of righteousness;

*All of us have become like one who is unclean, and all our righteous acts are the filthy rags; we all shrivel up like a leaf, and like the wind our sins sweep us away* (Isa.64:6).

*There is no one righteous, not even one* (Rom.3:10; Ps.14:1-3).

All these revelations helped the followers of the Bible to seek righteousness only from God. According to the Bible, every person, including prophets, are alike; they were born from sinful parents and are in need of salvation from God. The following verses of the Bible show the crying out of the king and prophet, David, who declares the unworthiness of his deeds and position before God as he begs for immediate salvation;

> *Wash away all my iniquity and cleanse me from my sins. For I know my transgressions, and my sin is always before me. Against you, you only, have I sinned and done what is evil in your sight, ...Surely I was sinful at birth, sinful from the time my mother conceived me... Create in me a pure heart, O God, and renew a steadfast spirit within me* (Ps.51:3-5,10).

It is foolish to rely on someone, who himself, like everyone else on the earth, is in desperate need of salvation from God. It is even more foolish to take the whole life and teaching of such a person as an absolute authority for how to live one's life on earth and the life after. That is why the Bible calls upon people not to obey invitations blindly, but to make sure whether they are right or wrong. In the Bible, every call is first directed to the minds of people for evaluation and examination so that people can distinguish between right and wrong. This is the way that biblical faith helps people to choose the way that enables them to walk in the true path. In the Bible, God even curses those who rely on true prophets as mediators for salvation;

> Then the LORD said to me: "Even if Moses and Samuel were to stand before me, my heart would not go out to these people (Jer.15:1).

> ...if a country sins against me...declares the sovereign LORD, even if Noah, Daniel and Job were in it, they could save neither son nor daughter. They would save only themselves by their righteousness (Eze.14:12,20).

> This is what the LORD says: "Cursed is the one who trusts in man, who depends on flesh for his strength...(Jer.17:5).

In biblical faith, the mediator cannot be one who is from the earth but must be someone who is in and from heaven (paradise). The job of the earthly prophet is to preach repentance and to beg for the intercessory work of the one in and from heaven. The one in and from heaven is a stranger to sin, and is in no need of repentance. That is why even the righteous ones of the earth are not able to intercede for the lives of others before God. This is because their own righteousness is the result of God's intercessory grace towards them after they repented and asked to be in the kingdom of God. The mediator, therefore, must be someone who is totally on God's side and has never sinned against God and people. This biblical testimony goes against the words of the Qur'an, that calls people to rely on Muhammad and on whatever he says and does. According to the Qur'an, Muhammad was a sinful man and thus in desperate need of a mediator;

> *And the burdened soul shall not bear the burden of another: and if the heavy laden soul cry out for its burden to be carried, yet shall not aught of it be carried, even by the near of kin!...(Q.35:18).*

> *...seek pardon for thy (Muhammad) fault...(Q.40:55; cf. 47:19; 48:2).*

## Teaching on Love and War

Muhammad stretched his mind toward heretical opinions about Jesus and started blaming the Christians, accusing them of misinterpreting the Bible. Even so, he still expected Christians to stay supportive of him despite all the changes in his direction, but they refused to welcome him anymore. That caused him to become angry and to change his friendly stance towards Christians to one of confrontation;

> *O believers! take not the Jews or Christians as friends. They are but one another's friends. If any one of you taketh them for his friends, he surely is one of them! God will not guide the evil doers (Q.5:51).*

*Whoso desireth any other religion than Islam, that religion shall never be accepted from him, and in the next world he shall be among the lost* (Q.3:85).

According to the words of Muhammad, those who do not believe in Islam must be severely punished in this world and no one should be able to support them;

*And as to those who believe not, I will chastise them with a terrible chastisement in this world and in the next; and none shall they have to help them* (Q.3:56).

This is a complete contradiction to the words of Jesus;

*But I tell you love your enemies and pray for those who persecute you, that you may be the sons of your Father in heaven. He causes his sun to rise on the evil and the good, and sends rain on the righteous and the unrighteous* (Matt.5:44-45).

Through the leadership of Jesus Christ, Christians see God as the source of "love" for all humankind regardless of their race, beliefs and nationalities. God proved His love through His revelation and atoning work in the Son, Jesus Christ. God did this in order to attract, save and return the lost to the state that existed before the fall. The Gospel of the Son teaches us;

*"...love comes from God. Everyone who loves has been born of God and knows God. Whoever does not love does not know God, because God is love. This is how God showed his love among us: He sent his one and only Son into the world that we might live through him. This is love: not that we loved God, but that he loved us and sent his Son as an atoning sacrifice for our sins... since God so loved us, we also ought to love one another. No one has ever seen God; but if we love one another, God lives in us and his love is made complete in us.*

*We know that we live in him and he in us, because he has given us his Spirit. And we have seen and testify that the Father has sent his Son to be the Saviour of the world. If anyone acknowledges that Jesus is the Son of God, God lives in him and he in God. And so we know and rely on the love God has for us.*

*God is love. Whoever lives in love lives in God, and God in him. In this way, love is made complete among us so that we will have confidence on the day of judgement, because in this world we are like him. There is no fear in love. But perfect love drives out fear, because fear has to do with punishment. The one who fears is not made perfect in love.*

*We love because he first loved us. If anyone says, "I love God," yet hates his brother, he is a liar. For anyone who does not love his brother, whom he has seen, cannot love God, whom he has not seen. And he has given us this command: Whoever loves God must also love his brother"* (1John4:7-21).

Love remains at the forefront of God's work for the world. He proved His love by sending His Son Jesus Christ to free the world from enmity and rebellion, reconciling the world to Himself. Love is perfect. It relates all things in heaven and earth to one another peacefully and in a perfect way. There is no law against love. That is why Christians call Jesus the Prince of peace and love, because he chose to love His enemies contrary to what his enemies did to him. With His love, Jesus is the real liberator of the world and he expresses the perfect law of liberty.

This is the example God Almighty desires the world to follow. He loves the world and wants people to follow His footsteps by loving and respecting one another. God created people with love and for love in order to relate them to one another in the same way He relates Himself to His creatures. God created people in spiritual likeness to Himself and blessed them in His love so they could become His fruitful agents on earth (Gen.1:26-28). That is why the essence and the central message of His word is love;

> *'Love the Lord your God with all your soul and with all your mind, ...and love your neighbor as yourself. All the law and the prophets hang on these two commandments'* (Matt.22:37-39; Deut.5:21-22; 6:5).

These words challenge people to engage their minds and hearts in understanding the depth, height and width of love in order to discover the status of their soul in relation to God and His creatures. They show us whether we are related to God and whether we are fully enabled to relate to the world around us. They are to make us godly and friendly people. The whole philosophy of the Bible is that, if we unite with Jesus Christ, we will no longer be slaves to narrow mindedness and separatist behaviours but we will be liberated in order to love God and to live in peace with His creatures.

Muslims, however, are not able to describe God in the same way that Christians do. The words of the Qur'an present Muslims as the ultimate community of God that must manifest the success of God through military force. Radical Muslims draw their fighting spirit from the teachings of the Qur'an, Muhammad and his successors and fight their non-Muslim neighbors instead of loving them;

> *Believers! wage war against such of the infidels as are your neighbors, and let them find you rigorous: and know that God is with those who fear him* (Q.9:123).

> *Make war upon such of those to whom the Scriptures have been given as believe not in God, or in the last day, and who forbid not that which God and His Apostle have forbidden, and who profess not the profession of the truth, until they pay tribute*

*out of hand, and they be humbled...The Jews say, 'Ezra is a son of God'; and the Christians say, 'the Messiah is a son of God.'...God do battle with them! How are they misguided (Q.9:29-30).*

## What Does It Mean To Be a Good Muslim?

The Qur'an says those Muslims who take part in the jihad for killing the non-Muslims are set apart in the eyes of Allah compared with those who do not join the jihad. They are considered superior to others;

*War is prescribed to you: but from this you are averse... (Q.2:216).*

*Those believers who sit at home free from trouble, and those who do valiantly in the cause of God with their substance and their persons, shall not be treated alike. God hath assigned to those who contend earnestly with their persons and with their substance, a rank above those who sit at home. Goodly promises hath He made to all. But God has assigned to the strenuous a rich recompense, above those who sit still at home (Q.4: 95).*

*They who were left at home were delighted to stay behind God's Apostle, and were averse from contending with their riches and their persons for the cause of God, and said,*

*'March not out in the heat.' SAY: A fiercer hat will be the fire of Hell.' Would that they understood this* (Q.9:81).

Therefore, the invasion of non-Muslims became the focal point of the faith of every true Muslim. Accordingly, invasions became the major tool for the spread of Islam and, in fact, spreading Islam became the main reason for going to war. In this way, Islam became the official religion of Arabia bringing every aspect of the life of the people under its control. Therefore, the teachings and acts of Muhammad and his successors caused Muslims, down through the centuries, to feel they had an obligation to wage battles and to inflict violence against non-Muslims.

To the fundamentalist Muslim, the population of the world is divided into two groups, Muslims (clean) and non-Muslims (unclean). According to the Qur'an, there can be no peace between these two groups. The Qur'an orders Muslims to kill those who worship other gods and who do not believe in Islam, until all the earth becomes subjected to the rule of Islam (dhimmitude – the English term that refers to the Islamic framework for treatment of conquered peoples);

*And when the sacred months are passed, kill those who join other gods with God wherever ye shall find them; and seize them, besiege them, and lay wait for them with every kind of ambush: but if they shall convert, and observe prayer, and pay the obligatory alms, then let them go their way, for God is Gracious, Merciful (Q.9: 5)*

*O Believers! Only they who join gods with God are unclean! Let them not, therefore, after this their year, come near the sacred Temple. And if ye fear want, God, if He pleases, will enrich you of His abundance: for God is Knowing, Wise. Make war upon such of those to whom the Scriptures have been given as believe not in God, or in the last day, and who forbid not that which God and His Apostle have forbidden, and who profess not the profession of the truth, until they pay tribute out of hand, and they be humbled (Q.2:28-29).*

*When you encounter the infidels, strike off their heads till ye have make a great slaughter among them, and of the rest make fast the fetters. And afterwards let there either be free dismissals or ransomings, till the war hath laid down its burdens. Thus do. Were such the pleasure of God, he could himself take vengeance upon them: but He would rather prove the one of you by the other. And whoso fight for the cause of God, their works he will not suffer to miscarry (Q.47:4).*

*Say to the infidels; If they desist from their unbelief, what is now past shall be forgiven*

*them; but if they return to it, they have
already before them the doom of the
ancients! Fight then against them till strife
be at an end, and the religion be all of it
God's. If they desist, verily God beholdeth
what they do* (Q.8:38-39).

*And remember when God promised you*
(Muslims) *that one of the two troops should
fall to you, and ye desired that they who had
no arms should fall to you: but God
purposed to prove true the truth of his
words, and to cut off the uttermost part of
the infidels* (Q.8:7).

However, a way out was provided for those Jews
and Christians who, in a sense, did not want to be
killed by Muslims. Their obligation to the Muslims
was that they had to abide by the Islamic laws and
pay a yearly amount (jizyah) to the Islamic ruler in
order to live;

*Make war upon such of those to whom the
Scripture have been given as believe not in
God, or in the last day, and who forbid not
that which God and His Apostle have
forbidden, and who profess not the
profession of the truth, until they pay tribute
out of hand, and they be humbled* (Q.9: 29).

The issue of tribute was not followed as prescribed
in the Qur'an all of the time. Its legitimacy has
depended very much on the various circumstances

in Islamic societies. Some have favored the use of pressure, persecution, terror and the like rather than getting tribute. Some favored less pressure and therefore preferred tribute. Some others preferred to ignore both.

However, a true Muslim is always called to stay faithful to the teaching of the Qur'an and Muhammad, fighting for the cause of Allah in the spreading of Islam. Even nominal Muslims unconsciously or consciously through their religious payments are indirectly involved in the war (jihad) against non-Muslims. The large amount of money that the religious leaders collect from the Muslim community is invested for the raising up of true Muslims who are called to fight for the cause of Allah. The giving of money is unavoidable for the majority of nominal Muslims. This is not solely because of the love they hold towards Islam, but because of the fear of evil spirits and the battles that are common in Islamic culture. Generally, people vow to pay to a mosque or to a saint's tomb. However, the giving is seen as part of their religious duty or obligation - a good deed that might bring comfort to its giver or might increase the possibility of the giver gaining entry into any desired situation, including paradise.

Each Muslim is called to safeguard their own life according to Islamic values and to try in any possible way to spread Islam among non-Islamic people.

# Fighting Freedom

The writings of the Qur'an and the history of Islam's growth have proven that Muslims must attempt to convert the world by using any tool; from the most gentle to the most ruthless. Islam does not leave people with the freedom to make their own religious decisions. The major strategic objective for faithful Muslims is to undermine the rights of every non-Islamic community in the world so that they cannot run their own societies according to their own cultural values. Wherever Islam has invaded, they have eliminated the current systems of those places, burnt the libraries and books of that society and imposed their authoritarian system over it.

In some Islamic countries, Islam was not imported through direct invasions, but through laymen evangelists. However, regardless of the entry process, the spirit of jihad was in the essence of Islam and could not be separated from it. The spirit of jihad rose up in any community where there was a majority of Muslims, thus causing violence, force and pressure to be the overriding focus of every fanatical Muslim against native non-Muslims.

Islam is a severe religion in practice. This severity has made it extraordinarily estranged from both giving and using freedom in its real sense. In fact, the word 'freedom' does not have an independent definition in the doctrine of Islam. It must always be defined in the shadow of Islam's fluctuating politics. That is why, in strongly religious oriented governments, freedom only means freedom to show allegiance to whatever the ruling government imposes on the residents. Ruling governments in Islamic countries who do respect and protect personal freedom, are not relying totally on Islam. They prefer to leave behind the severity of Islam and adopt non-Islamic values for their society. We have heard many times how fundamentalist Muslims in these countries criticize such ruling authorities, calling them Western agents and raising up riots against their tolerance towards other ideas.

There were two reasons for Ayatollah Khomeini's protest in the 1970's against the king of Iran. Firstly, he protested because of the king's failure to fully maintain Islamic values and secondly he accused the king of adapting Iran towards non-Islamic values, namely Western. The slogan 'down with the king' that the Ayatollah's followers were shouting in the streets was always accompanied with 'down with America' and 'down with Israel'. This was mainly because the Ayatollah believed the king was friendly with America and America was helping Israel to grow stronger. Although, like all other governments of the world, the king had problems in his rule over Iran, this was not the major reason for the riots in Iran at that time by fundamentalist Muslims. Their motivation was only to turn the non-religious government into a religious one and in this way to 'arrest and chain' freedom. But as became obvious after the revolution in Iran, Khomeini's first call was apparently for Iran to be freed from the dictatorship of the king of Iran, who, he asserted, was a Western agent. However, the calls he issued later were not in accord with his first call. His later calls showed that he wanted to establish a far stronger dictatorship and his rule became a threat towards other religions and ideas in Iran. One of his calls was to all of the Islamic scholars around the world, whom he wanted to undertake the destruction of all other religious centers other than Islam.[121] His successor Ali Khamnei also on another occasion called on many Islamic countries to prepare the ground for the creation of Islamic governments in all countries.[122] Similarly, what happened in Pakistan, Afghanistan, Indonesia, Sudan and in other Islamic countries against non-Muslims is in line with the objectives of Islam against freedom.

There are times in Islamic history where, to some extent, Muslims showed tolerance towards Christians and Jews. This tolerance was there only when the true followers of Islam did not have extensive religious power over the society. However, the issue of Islamic fundamentalism was always a matter of fear for non-Muslims throughout the history of Islam. Fundamentalist Muslim invasions against the rights of non-Muslims are the result of calls and motivations that arise out of Islam. Nominal Muslims, on the other hand, are

---

[121] M. Ayyubi (ed), *Khumeini Speaks Revelation,* (trans., N. M. Shaikh), Karachi: International Islamic Pub., 1981, P.25.
[122] S. Bakhash, *The Reign of the Ayatollahs: Iran and the Islamic Revolution*, New York: Basic Books, 1984, P.235.

more tolerant and respectful toward the rights of others from different religious backgrounds, because they are less dependent on the calls of their religion.

The spirit of violence, force and pressure found in Islamic doctrine can be traced back to the very beginning of Muhammad's faith. You will remember from an earlier chapter that an angelic revelation was the starting point for Muhammad. The tradition says the following about this encounter. The angel Gabriel forced him to read the first verses of the Qur'an, while he was illiterate. The angel caught him forcefully and pressed him three times so hard, up to the point that his neck muscles twitched with terror. After the angel read the verses, Muhammad had no other choice but to repeat the angel's words.[123] The spirit of Islam is the spirit of war and pressure any time it enters an individual's life or a society. It may be a silent or a riotous entry, but it always adapts and prepares Muslims gradually so that they ultimately express a spirit of fighting against non-Muslims.

Muhammad and his community believed in Jihad for the establishment of God's kingdom on the earth. In contrast God's kingdom as taught by Jesus is not of this world;

---

[123] Ibn Hisham, *Sirat Rasul Allah,* P.209. & Also, read the narratives in Phil Parshall, *Inside the Community,* PP.18-21.

*Jesus said, "My kingdom is not of this world. If it were, my servants would fight to prevent my arrest by the Jews. But my kingdom is from another place* (John 18:36: cf. Isa.9:6-7).

His disciple, Paul, said;

*Be careful, however, that the exercise of your freedom does not become a stumbling block to the weak* (1Cor.8:9).

The Bible says that the kingdom of heaven can not be established by the sword and by the shedding of the blood of humankind;

*"Put your sword back in its place" Jesus said...*(Matt.26:52).

*For our struggle is not against flesh and blood...*(Eph.6:12).

Therefore, the kingdom of God was established by God's love when Jesus took His stand to reconcile the world to God through love, against the devil's schemes of hatred, discord, fits of rage and the like;

*He* (God) *rescued us from the dominion of darkness and brought us into the kingdom of the Son he loves,...For God was pleased to have all his fullness dwell in him, and through him to reconcile to himself all things, whether things on earth or things in heaven, by making peace through his blood, shed on the cross* (Col.1:13,20).

*The acts of the sinful nature are obvious: sexual immorality, impurity and debauchery, idolatry and witchcraft; hatred, discord, jealousy, fits of rage, selfish ambition, dissensions, factions and envy; drunkenness, orgies, and the like...But the fruit of the Spirit is love, joy, peace, patience, kindness, goodness, faithfulness, gentleness and self-control. Against such things there is no law. Those who belong to Christ Jesus have crucified the sinful nature with its passions and desires* (Gal.5:19-24).

As is obvious, the kingdom of the Son Jesus Christ is represented by "love", whereas the kingdom of Muhammad is represented by the "sword". This grave and profound difference between Christian and Islamic doctrine has been causing Christians to suffer ever since the rise of Islam as a state religion. Muhammad announced himself as the absolute prophet for all and called all people, no matter whether they were monotheists or polytheists, to put their beliefs aside, even if good, and believe in Islam;

*SAY to them: O men! Verily I am God's apostle to you all;...the unlettered prophet... And follow him that ye may be guided aright* (Q.7:158).

As a result of this, Christians and Jews also were asked to believe in Muhammad's new religion;

> *The true religion with God is Islam:...*
> *Abraham was neither Jew nor Christian; but*
> *he was sound in the faith, a Muslim;... Other*
> *religion than that of God desire they?...*
> *Whoso desireth any other religion than*
> *Islam, that religion shall never be accepted*
> *from him, and in the next world he shall be*
> *among the lost* (Q.3:19,67,83,85).

Those Christians and Jews who did not believe in Muhammad's message and did not join him or departed from him, were called enemies to Islam and consequently subject to death unless they signed a treaty and paid some tribute in order to live.   In this way, those Christians and Jews who lived under the domination of Islam, became subject to different kinds of attacks and threats from the rise of Islam till now (cf. Q.5:51; 9:29-30). Their beliefs and lives came to be seen as worthless and unlawful in the eyes of Islamic people, merely because they chose not to submit to Islam.   They were treated as strangers in their own lands and hometowns, and therefore, were killed or forced to pay tribute or leave.[124]

---

[124] For further information read Colin Chapman, PP.283-289; quotations from Islamic traditions and contemporary writings.

So Islam became an authoritarian religion and every one had to bow down before it. Those who did not embrace it Muhammad stamped as infidels and did everything he could to convert them either by persuasion or by force.[125] As has happened with other authoritarian political systems throughout history, Islamic leaders searched for various excuses in order to legitimize the wiping out of those who thought differently and held other beliefs. Christians and Jews were not immune from the impact of these excuses. Muhammad held the contemporary Arabian Jews responsible for all the wrongdoing that the Jewish nation had committed from the exodus till the rise of Islam and he charged them with unbelief, mainly because they did not accept his prophecy. Similarly, Christians also suffered persecution under Islam but in a different way. Muhammad was aware of the tension between Jews and Christians. Christians accused Jews of rejecting Jesus and killing the prophets and Jews accused Christians of blasphemy for calling Jesus the Son of God. Muhammad too used the same accusations in his approach to Jews and Christians.

Another excuse to blame Christians was through using heretical Christian beliefs from church history. For example, there were always heretical beliefs, as early as the first century AD that spread to people from different nations and posed a threat to real Christianity. These heresies denied the deity,

---

[125] K. Savage, P.122.

sonship and crucifixion of Jesus Christ.[126] These kinds of heretical ideas would have been familiar to Muhammad and some of his companions, because heretics were living everywhere Christians lived. An ancient Muslim researcher, who collected information from various religions and ideas for his book, wrote about the wide spread heretical Christian beliefs in Muhammad's time and explained why the Qur'an spoke negatively of two Christian sects, the Malkanites and Jacobites.[127] These heretical Christian ideas were used by Muslims to justify action by the law of the sword against Christianity. Christians were forced to acknowledge Muhammad's point of view, reducing the divine position of Jesus Christ to the level of his own politico-religious position. As a result, Christians were purged out of Arabia.

The success resulting from the war and violence against non-Islamic territories caused Islam's spirit of war and violence to become more impetuous and covetous, seeing the whole world as its territory for invasion, in order to overcome all opponents. Ever since the rise of the Islamic state, the spirit of war and violence within Islam has been wanting to invade every person in the world, who for any reason dared to become critical towards Islam. Fundamental Muslims have always seen critics of their movement as an invasion of Islam's universal

---

[126] ISB Encyclopedia, under the word 'Heresy', PP.684-6.
[127] A. M. A. Shahrestani, *Tozih-almelal*, PP.344,351 from book1.

territory, and have called Muslims to target those who expressed the criticism, no matter what territorial rights and laws were in place to protect these individuals.

**Teaching on Free Will**

The same pressures that the people of Mecca exerted on Muhammad and which he opposed, have unfortunately become the distinguishing characteristic of Muslim culture ever since Islam emerged as the state religion. Meccans accused Muhammad of disregarding the religion of his forefathers;

> *For when our distinct signs are recited to them, they say, 'This is merely a man who would fain pervert you from your father's worship.' And they say, 'This* (Koran) *is no other than a forged falsehood.' And the unbelievers say to the truth when it is presented to them, 'Tis nothing but palpable sorcery'* (Q.34:43).

Later when Muhammad had succeeded, he treated others who drew back from Islam, deserting the faith, in a harsher manner than the Meccan's had treated him;

> *O believers! make not friends of your fathers or your brethren if they love unbelief above*

*faith: and whoso of you shall make them his friends, will be wrong doers* (Q.9:23).

*O ye who believe! Verily, in your wives and your children ye have an enemy: wherefore beware of them. But if ye pass it over and pardon, and are lenient, then God is too Lenient, Merciful* (Q.64:14).

*Give not way therefore to the Infidels, but by means of this Koran strive against them with a mighty strife* (Q.25:52).

*O Prophet! make war on the infidels and hypocrites, and deal rigorously with them...* (Q.66:9).

Abubakr, Muhammad's successor (first caliphite) and father-in-law, who accompanied Muhammad when he invaded a Meccan Caravan, became eager to shed the blood of his own son, Abdurahman, who did not accept Islam and had come with the Meccan warriors to protect the caravan. He called his son a villain and impure and demanded back the portion of his wealth he had given his son. The son replied, 'why are you asking for wealth while the sword exists between you and me?' The incident turned into a bloody battle called Badre. At the beginning of the war, his son dared someone to fight him one on one and Abubakre accepted the challenge. When he realized it was his father that stepped forward, Abdurahman withdrew as a sign of respect.[128]

Ali, the forth caliphate and the holy leader of the Shiite sect, said, 'Allah has commanded war against those who desert Islam'.[129]

## One Way Freedom

Muhammad believed in his freedom to leave his inherited religion behind, but didn't believe in the freedom of Muslims to leave Islam. He started his ministry by satirizing the leaders and their idols in Mecca, but never allowed others to question his deeds or religion. This 'one way' expression of freedom penetrated institutions and individuals and ever since they have been aggressive towards those who left the Muslim religion in Islamic societies. It also has become a lurking and dangerous value in Islam's social and judiciary system, resulting in waves of assault against other cultures and beliefs. The limitation or banning of the activities of minor religions, the closure of their worship places and printing houses and the imprisonment and killing of their believers and leaders are all the result of this 'one way' expression of freedom in Islam.

In Islamic culture, no one has the right to question any part of Islam. 'Rational ethics or political

---

[128] Ibn Hisham, *Sirat Rasul Allah*, P.575.
[129] Salim Ibn-Ghaisse, *Asrar Aal Muhammad*, P.88.

science or economic theory- as the product of human logic, argumentation, dialectic or pondered experience - theoretically do not exist in Islam...Man is not meant to argue for democracy'.[130] Yet, as a Muslim entering societies (big or small) in non-Islamic nations, you have the right to use or abuse the freedoms that those nations have provided at a great price. Furthermore, your Islamic faith gives you the right to even humiliate the values of your host society. In contrast, when it comes to the Islamic arena, you are requested to show blind allegiance to the Islamic Nation. Islamic authorities prescribe limitless rights anytime, anywhere, anyway and over anybody to faithful Muslims, but when it comes to non-Muslims or even faithless Muslims the leaders never leave any space for them to express or exercise their rights. These kinds of values and beliefs have become a strong part of the national culture of many Muslim communities.

Within the history of Islam leaders of Islamic communities have believed it is their right to continually criticize, attack and discredit the Christian faith, books and beliefs. But a fundamentalist Muslim believes that a person who criticizes, attacks or discredits Islamic belief, must be put to death. If the person is out of the reach of Islamic authorities, they look to terrorists to kill the person in exchange for a money reward.

---

[130] K. Cragg, P. 143.

Islam sees itself as having an open door only to those things that strengthen the Muslim community against non-Muslims. For example, in order to empower Muslims, purchasing weapons even from one's enemies is lawful. Any fighting methods used by outsiders are legitimate and may be learnt and put into practice, no matter what the cost. To strengthen the fighting spirit, gambling on shooting contests is lawful under Islam. Approaches to living in peace with non-Muslims or even with faithless Muslims are not considered or accepted.

Words like "democracy" and "freedom" are used in Islamic societies, but they have no meaning for those who do not contribute to the growth of Islam. In nominal Islamic societies, the freely elected governments and leaders, elected by the majority of votes, are under threat of assassination by fundamentalists who are angered that the government shows respect for the free will of the people. This kind of pressure from fundamentalists has caused nominal Muslim governments in almost all Islamic countries to unwillingly show favor towards fundamentalists. This has resulted in the rights of other minorities being ignored. This type of behavior by democratically elected governments has been necessary to gain momentum for the political survival of governments.

## No Freedom of Speech

In an Islamic society, when religious values dominate all relationships, it even becomes dangerous to explore the paradoxical words of a religious leader.

When Ayatollah Khomeini returned to Iran in 1979, he gave his first speech in a famous cemetery in the capital city, Tehran. His aim in choosing this place was to assert that the Shah had not brought progress to the country but had only brought progress to this cemetery by killing his opposition. Using this as an object lesson he indirectly promised he, contrary to the Shah's regime, would build the country and not the cemetery. This speech was powerful and had a positive effect on the people of Iran both emotionally and politically. However a few years later, after gaining power for his regime, he himself became a 'super slaughtering power' in Iran and made the cemetery ten times bigger than ever before. The country slipped backwards but the cemetery went forwards! This, of course, contradicted his first speech held in the cemetery, but no one had the right to criticize him!

While I was living in my home country, in one of my speeches I put forward the proposition that, for the benefit of the society, any wrong doing by any one must not be ignored. Rather the person doing these wrong acts, who might even be the leader of the country, must be advised. I considered myself very lucky when I was able to escape the death penalty for making this speech. I only managed to do this by being accepted as a refugee in a non-Islamic country.

I can give you another example but this time from a minor Islamic community in a Christian country. An English man had an appointment with this ethnic community to discuss some issues. He was asked if he could arrange to bring along an interpreter, as this would help them to communicate together confidently. This person called me and asked for my help as an interpreter. I went with him and performed the task of interpreter. At the meeting there were two males from the community present, along with the English man and myself as interpreter. The discussion went on for a while and the two men decided that we needed a five-minute break for a cup of tea. In the tea-time, they started talking to me in their own language. During our discussion they discovered that I was a Muslim who had converted to Christianity. Hearing this, they both paused for a few seconds and informed me that they didn't need me as an interpreter anymore. I reminded them that the meeting had not finished yet. They agreed that was the case, but they were not interested in working with an interpreter who could not keep his forefathers religion. Whatever we tried to say to them (the English man and myself) in an effort to continue the second part of the discussion with them didn't work. They weren't interested because of my conversion to Christianity. The English man asked them what was their motivation for breaching the right of equal opportunity and freedom in this country by refusing to work with me as an interpreter? He asked them to give a reason why they as Muslims were happy to use the freedoms given to them by non-Muslims but were not happy to give any freedom to others. He then said 'According to the law of this country, we have been discriminated against by you'. 'Do I have the right to call the police here or not?' he asked them. They did not answer his questions. The only thing they said to him in their broken English was, 'we need you come another time.' They both turned their faces towards me and said to me in their own language; 'you are unclean, are you going to leave the building or do you want us to kick you out?' They did not want to stay face to face with me anymore. Their pleasure was only to be found in my departure. In short, we both left.

Apparently, they both did not seem to be fundamentalist Muslims. However, as leaders of the community, they might have felt obligated to carry out the views of the community. This kind of *fanatical mindset* makes it difficult for some Muslims to accept the reality that people have freedom of choice in God's eyes.

Political, economic and social pressures were made legitimate in fundamentalist Islamic societies, in order to keep Muslims far from any opportunity for conversion. People are pushed to withdraw entirely from any Western model for society. That includes moving away from the freedom to uphold human rights with the loss of any respect for universal human rights. People are driven to become consistent in the practice of the Islamic way of life only.

This lack of freedom in Islamic culture has left it far behind in terms of meeting the natural needs of human life. There is always an uncertain and an insecure feeling for every Muslim who becomes interested in sharing thoughts and opinions with non-Muslims, and living in peace with them.

## The Love That Restores Peace

This lack of freewill and choice is in direct contrast to the will of God revealed in the Bible. God took the initiative to restore peace and acceptance among people by giving Himself as an example through the love of His Son Jesus Christ. In God's paradigm, love abounds regardless of allegiance;

> *"You have heard that it was said, 'Love your neighbor and hate your enemy.' But I tell you: Love your enemies and pray for those who persecute you, that you may be sons of your Father in heaven. He causes his sun to rise on the evil and the good, and sends rain on the righteous and the unrighteous. If you love those who love you, what reward will you get? Are not even the tax collectors doing that? And if you greet your brothers, what are you doing more than others? Do*

*not even pagans do that? Be perfect, therefore, as your heavenly Father is perfect* (Matt.5:43-48).

The courage for loving others finds its power in the Cross, where all the iniquities and inhuman activities of humankind were nailed so that the spirit of real freedom and love might be planted into the human heart. The faith of the Son Jesus Christ respects the choice and free will of people. He believes that spiritual freedom requires the practice of free will through investigation and discovering the truth (John 8:32) that restores peace.

## Teaching on Uniqueness of God

It is curious to note that the Qur'an itself, although it defends the unity of Allah and attributes the work of creation to him alone in many places (cf. Q.2:255; 6:101; 13:16; 112:1-4), seems indecisive in rejecting the idea of *"other creators"*;

> ... *Blessed therefore be God, the most excellent of Makers* (Q.23:14).

This verse clearly attributes the work of creation to the other idols as well and then calls Allah the best creator amongst all other creators. This can be taken to mean that although Allah is not the creator of all creatures, he is the best creator among the multiple creators. It could be for the same reason that in many places in the Qur'an, Allah is referred to in plural form, by the pronoun "we" rather than the singular "I". This plurality, for whatever reason it is used, cannot rest easily with Islam's practice of rigid and inflexible monotheism. In Islam, plurality of any kind (whether as a sign of respect and power or as a word for describing God's personalities) brings the absolute unity of Allah under question. For the Muslim, Allah is absolutely unique in his creation, in his revelation and in anything he wills and does. No one is allowed to say that there are multiple personalities in Allah. 'For Muslim theologians God has no (knowable) essence or nature from which one can distinguish his persons.'[131]

## Unique, but not in Revelation

As the evidence shows, the overall theology of the Qur'an is brought under question by its many paradoxical verses. Again as we have seen earlier, the revelation that there were various contradicting early manuscripts of the Qur'an in Islam's history is also another problem that makes the absolute unity of Allah impossible. Among the early manuscripts of the Qur'an, there was no absolute unity that was evident. Therefore, this lack of unity among the manuscripts proves that the source of this revelation was not unique. Muslims say that Muhammad's successor, Othman, selected the true revelation of Allah. However, Islamic absolutism

---

[131] N.L. Geisler & A. Saleeh, P.135.

does not allow any one to discern the absolute revelation from a group of revelations, especially if the person is not a prophet. Even Muhammad had trouble distinguishing the right from the wrong verses, and allowed both versions to be used.

Furthermore, as was mentioned above, Muhammad's own successors and early Islamic theologians attributed a few words of idol exaltation to Muhammad and asserted that he used these words some times in his prophetic ministry. This comes in sharp contradiction to the Qur'an's own saying about the complete and enduring faithfulness of the Jewish messengers, whereby they worshipped the only existing God and rejected idol exaltation;

> *And ask our Sent Ones whom we have sent before thee, 'Appointed we gods beside the God of Mercy whom they should worship?* (Q.43:45).

## Unique, but not in Worshipping

Again in another area, we can see that Muhammad stood in favor of maintaining the practices and desires of pagan converts to Islam, when he authenticated the pilgrimage to Mecca and the custom of bowing before a black stone and kissing it, all of which belonged to pre-Islamic idolatrous rituals (Q.2:158; 22:26-27). Worshipping and kissing a stone appear to be idolatrous and lawless acts and therefore oppose the monotheistic view of God presented in Islamic theology. "God and idolatry are incompatible."[132]

How do these unforgivable words, thoughts and acts carried out by Muhammad come to be forbidden for everyone else, but remain as acceptable for the prophet? He blamed the people of the Book for going beyond the truth and yet he was not able to avoid this himself;

> O ye people of the Book! Overstep not bounds in your religion; and of God speak only truth... (Q.4:171).

How can a system of thought criticize others for their sins, while it has condoned the same sins in its sacred writings? Why do Muslim leaders and writers pay no attention to their own sin recorded in their holy book but still condemn others and very often give formal orders to kill others by accusing them of the same sin?

The main reason for this problem is in the nature of Islam. Islam has not allowed itself to be advised by the most valuable source of advice - namely self-criticism regarding one's approach to others. Jesus Christ strongly urges self-examination before judgment of others. Truly, the name "Jesus" or "The Son" is the only way that all the nations of the world can be rightly united to each other, because

---

[132] K. Cragg, P.38.

his is the way of love. This unity cannot be achieved unless people follow the humble steps and advice of Jesus Christ. It is here again that the Qur'an and the Bible differ from each other when Jesus says;

*"How can you say to your brother, 'Let me take the speck out of your eye, 'when all the time there is plank in your own eye? You hypocrite, first take the plank out of your own eye, and then you will see clearly to remove the speck from your brother's eye"* (Matt.7:45).

## Teaching on the Crucifixion

There are two different statements about the death and crucifixion of Jesus in the Qur'an and tradition[133];

One statement refers to God's plan to put Jesus to death and thereafter to take Him back to heaven;

*Remember when God said, 'O Jesus! verily I will cause thee to die, and will take thee up to myself and deliver thee from those who believe not* (Q.3:55).

*And the peace of God was on me* (Jesus) *the day I was born, and will be the day I shall*

---

[133] Tabari, Muhammad-bin Jarir, *Tarikh-al-rosol val-molouk,* PP.520-21.

*die, and the day I shall be raised to life* (Q.19: 33).

But there is an opposing statement in the Qur'an, that says Jesus was neither killed nor crucified but simply taken to God;

> *And for their saying, 'Verily we have slain the Messiah, Jesus the son of Mary, and Apostle of God.' Yet they slew him not, and they crucified him not, but they had only his likeness. And they who differed about him were in doubt concerning him: No sure knowledge had they about him, but followed only an opinion, and they did not really slay him, but God took him up to Himself. And God is Mighty, Wise!* (Q.4:157-158).

The footnote of the editor of an ancient Muslim scholar's book also confirms the death of Christ by referring to three first century non-Christian historians, Josephus, Tacitus (Tacit) and Suetonius (Suetone).[134]

However, in describing the life of Jesus Christ on earth, Muslims rely on Q.4:157-158. They do not believe that Jesus was crucified or that Jesus died on the cross for the sin of all people before rising again. They do believe that one of those who plotted to kill Jesus died in his place. They state that God

---

[134] Shahrestani, A. M. A., *Tozih-almelal*, P.316 of book1.

took Jesus into heaven at that time and changed another man's face to look like Jesus. Although the man was shouting that he was not Jesus, no one listened to him and he was substituted for Jesus and put to death on the cross.

Muslims believe Muhammad is too holy to be likened by men. An example is when Muslims did not allow Hollywood to show 'Muhammad's' face in the film, "Muhammad, the Apostle of Allah". Considering that the Qur'an introduced Jesus as sinless and greatest among all the prophets, including Muhammad, why would Muslims venerate Muhammad and not Jesus? What was the purpose of making a Jesus look alike die and taking the unique Jesus to heaven? Wouldn't it have been better for God not to deceive people but rather kill off His enemies and take Jesus to heaven before the eyes of the people?

As we are aware from Church History, the idea of the substitution of somebody else for Christ on the cross is not unique to Islam. In fact, it goes back to centuries before Islam. From the second century AD, some people said that Jesus could not have been crucified and that somebody else was crucified in his place.

There are many reasons for why these substitution legends are not historically credible:[135]

---

[135] Read N.L. Geisler & A. Saleeh, PP.280-6.

- The Gospel says that Jesus was crucified.

- There are extra-biblical testimonies about the death of Christ.

- There is not a shred of first-century testimony to the contrary by friend or foe of Christianity.

- The legends ignore the participation of Jesus' disciples, and of the Romans who crucified him.

Muslims denial of Christ's death by crucifixion is based on their misunderstandings of biblical theology.

This belief that Jesus went straight into heaven, still raises some theological questions, which may help Muslims to realize some great facts about Jesus: Why would Jesus, and not Muhammad, be taken to the heavenly place to be with God? Why would Muhammad not be certain about himself being one day with God, whereas he was about Jesus?;

> *SAY: I have no control over what may be helpful or hurtful to me, but as God willeth. Had I the knowledge of his secrets, I should revel in the good, and evil should not touch me...* (Q.7:188).

*SAY: I am no apostle of new doctrines: neither know I what will be done with me or you...* (Q.46:9).

If Muhammad was the seal of the prophets, why wasn't he sure of being in heavenly places like Jesus who, according to Muslims, is a lesser prophet? Why did he not have the same hope and assurance as the prophets of the Bible? If he was not an apostle of a new doctrine and was following the same doctrine that the Son Jesus Christ followed, he should have been assured about his and his followers' salvation just like the followers of Christ;

*And this is the testimony: God has given us eternal life, and this life is in his Son. He who has the Son has life; he who does not have the Son of God does not have life* (1John5:11-12).

This is the confidence that the followers of the Son Jesus Christ have in their approach to God. The verbs "has given" and "has" in the verses above imply the assurance of salvation that they have in this life on earth. Muhammad himself also was aware of the certainty of salvation that comes by following Jesus Christ when he said;

*... God said,...I will place those who follow thee* (Jesus) *above those who believe not, until the day of resurrection* (Q.3:55-56).

Why would the Qur'an assert such a righteous position for the followers of Jesus but not for the followers of Muhammad? What is it that has made the name 'Jesus' a name that is above all other prophets? It is nothing other than the doctrine of 'the death and the resurrection of Jesus' that can provide the right answer to these questions. The atoning death and resurrection of Jesus Christ is the central theme of the Bible and it is this that has provided assurance of salvation for people. It opens the door of eternal life to humankind and brings them back to their original state of righteousness. The Cross is the basis of God's plan to reconcile people with God before their physical death on earth. It was in this way that the followers of Jesus became able to understand God's secrets, turning into a powerful tool for calling their enemies and the enemies of God to reconciliation with God. The Apostle Paul was initially one of the strictest enemies of Christians, and Jesus revealed the true secrets of life to him, thereby changing his life. The following words prove the life changing power of the Gospel of the Son Jesus Christ in Paul's life;

*All this is from God, who reconciled us to himself through Christ and gave us the ministry of reconciliation* (2Cor.5:18).

*"No eye has seen, no ear has heard, no mind has conceived what God has prepared for those who love him" but God has revealed it to us by his Spirit. The Spirit searches all things, even the deep things of God. For who*

*among men knows the thoughts of a man except the man's spirit within him? In the same way no one knows the thoughts of God except the Spirit of God. We have not received the spirit of the world but the Spirit who is from God, that we may understand what God has freely given us. This is what we speak, not in words taught us by human wisdom but in words taught by the Spirit, expressing spiritual truths in spiritual words. The man without the Spirit does not accept the things that come from the Spirit of God, for they are foolishness to him, and he cannot understand them, because they are spiritually discerned. The spiritual man makes judgements about all things, but he himself is not subject to any man's judgement: "For who has known the mind of the Lord that he may instruct him?" But we have the mind of Christ* (1Cor.2:9-16).

## Eternal Death versus the Death of Christ

It is not only the Son Jesus Christ that knows the secrets of the Kingdom of heaven. They are also revealed to those who follow Him. Through the atoning death of the Son, the followers of the Son also become the children of the Kingdom of heaven. The simple and understandable logic that lies behind being the children of God is that nothing of the Kingdom of heaven is hidden to its children. The children are not strangers. They know their heavenly Father's secrets. The death of the Son on the Cross and His resurrection from the dead have changed the spiritual identity of His followers. They have been moved from the kingdom of Satan to the Kingdom of heaven so that they can share in the knowledge and advantages of eternal life.

The death of the Son on the Cross is the sacrifice of God for the sin of the world. The resurrection of the Son is the victory of God over the eternal death of Satan. Eternal life is for those who are accepted and included in the price paid by God for our sin and share in the victory gained by Him through the Son Jesus Christ. In fact, this is the major difference between the Qur'an and the Bible. The words of the Qur'an do not reveal that any price was paid so that humankind could come back to God, and yet this theme is central in the Bible's revelation. The death of Jesus Christ is the necessary sacrifice for the sins of the world and His resurrection is the victory over eternal death. The theology of the Old and New Testaments is based upon the promise and realization of these events;

> *Surely he took up our infirmities and carried our sorrows... Yet it was the LORD's will to crush him and cause him to suffer, and though the LORD makes his life a guilt offering, he will see his offspring and prolong his days, and the will of the LORD will prosper in his hand. After the suffering of his soul, he will see the light of life, and be satisfied; by his knowledge my righteous*

*servant will justify many, and he will bear their iniquities* (Isa.53:6,10-11).

*He was delivered to death for our sins and was raised to life for our justification* (Rom.4:25).

*He himself bore our sins in his body on the tree, so that we might die to sins and live for righteousness; by his wounds you have been healed. For you were like sheep going astray, but now you have returned to the Shepherd and Overseer of your souls* (1Pet.2:24-25).

## The Finished Work of Christ

We know from the Qur'an that Muhammad blamed Jews for the killing of the prophets. In the Qur'an Jesus is also called a prophet! Why was it difficult for Muhammad to believe that the Jews also killed Jesus? What happened so that he changed his mind about Jesus' death and said that he never truly died? He might have heard about *"the finished work of Christ on the Cross"* from the contemporary Christians around him, and for that reason, he might have changed his mind. Why? Because the finished work of Christ on the Cross, in a sense, stands in opposition to Muhammad's assertion that his ministry was the final fulfillment of the prophetic task. This certainly could be one reason for him rejecting the teaching about the Cross.

Another reason might have been the fact that in Islam Jesus was called one of the five great prophets: Noah, Abraham, Moses, Jesus and Muhammad. If the Muslims' most powerful prophet, who led their political religion, confirmed that the tiny Jewish nation had dared to kill the greatest prophet (Jesus, who was in the same rank as Muhammad), it would have been very discouraging for the politico-religious army of Islam. This might have in turn led Muhammad to claim that the Jews killed the minor prophets, but not the ones in whom God placed so much love. Alternatively, Muhammad might have been discouraged by the Roman political belief that any crucified person had to be a criminal and therefore Christians worshipped a criminal and his cross. This kind of political belief opposes the religious values of Islam that assert that a prophet is holy and cannot be a criminal. It would have been another cause for Muhammad's rejection of the crucifixion.

## Righteousness through the Sacrifice of Christ

The philosophy that lies behind the crucifixion of the Son Jesus Christ is crucial to Christianity. Just as the descendants of Adam became unrighteous through his rebellious example, so also through the sacrifice of Jesus Christ on the cross many will follow Him and be made righteous (Rom.5:19). 'Why did Jesus undertake this task?' It was because God loves the world and wanted to have many in the world back in His kingdom. What Jesus did on the Cross was the result of God's love, justice and holiness directed towards the sinful world. This act made salvation available for the world.

Any understanding about Jesus is based on the relationship between the Cross and the forgiveness of sin in the Bible. Although Muhammad at some stages of his ministry accepted the truth about the death and the resurrection of Jesus Christ (Q.3:55; 19:33), he rejected it later on in his ministry and substituted something else in its place that could suit the progress of Islam (Q.4:157-158; 5:117).

## Teaching on Morality

Theologically speaking, Islam's own doctrine has left Muslims in the situation of not being able to recognize any ethical code and standard that represents the attributes of God. Why is this? As was discussed earlier, God has been introduced to Muslims as an unknowable God. Therefore, the truth and the goodness of God, as a potential standard for moral values, have been made inaccessible and unknowable to Muslims. Consequently, they are not able to have a real and godly code of ethics for comparing, evaluating and measuring the moral values of other nations. As a result, they are unable to claim any ethical supremacy over other beliefs and values.

This puts Muslims in a position that is out of step with human history. History shows that every person by nature is dynamic and has the potential to be open to learning and growth. However, Islam's doctrine has ignored the natural needs of humans and has closed the door to Muslims being dynamic and open about life. Muslims can only learn and grow within the framework presented by their leaders.

Also, a brief scrutiny of what the Qur'an teaches about life on earth and after death for its followers proves that an Islamic life style cannot be a morally good example for the world. The Qur'an does not believe that Muslims are in the kingdom of heaven (or paradise) in their life on earth as believers. Someone not in the kingdom of heaven cannot claim to be more morally trustworthy than the followers of other religions. Even the simplest logic shows that those who are truly in the kingdom of heaven must be examples of godly living for those who are not yet in heaven. It is possibly because of this recognized superior quality that the Qur'an itself places the true followers of Jesus Christ above others as morally perfect examples for the world. Consider the following verse that exalts Christians over all others, including Muslims;

> ... God said,...I will place those who follow thee (Jesus) above those who believe not, until the day of resurrection (Q.3:55-56).

Surely, the word 'above' points to the victorious spiritual life that Christians have gained through their faith in Jesus Christ, but Muslims are blinded to this truth in the Qur'an. Do Muslims themselves have such a victorious spiritual life through obedience to Muhammad that results in moral perfection?

We know that morality is a key issue for the life on earth. According to the verse above, in the entire world only true Christians are morally above all others who do not follow Jesus. Therefore, when the Qur'an supports the Christian conquest over unbelief, this should help Muslims to follow in the footsteps of Jesus rather than of Muhammad. This should be clear to any Muslim who chooses to read the Qur'an carefully and thoughtfully.

A third reason to reject the Islamic moral example is the two different positions that Muhammad and Jesus hold toward sin. According to the Qur'an, Jesus is sinless but Muhammad is a sinner. Therefore, the example of Jesus, introduced in the Qur'an, is perfect and better than the example of Muhammad. This in turn raises two other issues, which are worthy of consideration. Firstly, Jesus as the perfect model would never encourage people to follow any imperfect model. Secondly, Jesus would never let His perfect ministry be followed up by an imperfect ministry, especially when it is uncertain about salvation. Therefore, Muhammad's claim on calling himself the seal of the prophets contradicts the highest quality the Qur'an has attributed to

Jesus amongst all other prophets, including Muhammad himself.

The greatest mistake of Islam is its requirement of Muslims to be morally good examples for the world without noticing that they are not yet saved to undertake this great responsibility. Muslims are called to devote themselves to prayer five times a day in order to gain the favour of Allah and his forgiveness for the life after. This means that they are not forgiven (saved) yet. Even the most devoted Muslim is unsure of gaining 100 per cent forgiveness. Islam deprives its followers of the certainty of forgiveness. Whereas in Christianity, complete forgiveness *is* attainable and is the basis for God's moral law to be practiced in the lives of his followers. One must be dressed with the certainty of salvation like the true followers of Jesus Christ in order to become a good example for others. Paul, the disciple of Jesus Christ, said;

> (Our) *names are in the book of life. Our citizenship is in heaven* (Phil.4:3c; 3:20a).

> *When you were dead in your sins and in the uncircumcision of your sinful nature, God made you alive with Christ. He forgave us all our sins, having canceled the written code, with its regulations, that was against us and that stood opposed to us; he took it away, nailing it to the cross. And having disarmed the powers and authorities, he*

> *made public spectacle of them, triumphing over them by the cross* (Col.2:13-15).

Without this, no amount of effort will produce moral lives that are pleasing to God.

## The Breath of Debauchery

The criticism by Muslim evangelists of the Christian faith becomes more illogical when the author of their own faith, Allah, has ordained men and women to be sinners;

> *And* (God) *breathed into it* (human soul) *its wickedness* (which means debauchery) *and its piety* (Q.91:8).

Allah himself, in this way, has disabled them so that they are unable to escape their immorality. This does not match at all with the characteristics of the God of the Bible, which says;

> *God did not call us to be impure, but to live a holy life* (1Thes.4:7).

As a result, Islam has been unsuccessful in distinguishing truth from untruth about its doctrines throughout the history of Islam. It has encouraged its followers to escape immorality, but how can you escape what Allah has breathed into you?

The corruption of Islamic morality is revealed by the way Islamic religious leaders have documented copious embarrassing words about the private parts of females (as young as infants), talking about them as if they are objects and not human beings.[136]

We also learn from the Qur'an itself that women are not compelled to guard their private parts from their fathers, father-in-laws, their own sons or stepsons, brothers, nephews, slaves or even their sterilized male attendants. They also can show their private parts to children who have not yet shown any interest in women's nakedness;

> *And speak to the believing women that they refrain their eyes, and observe continence; and that they display not their ornaments, except those which are external; and that they throw their veils over their bosoms, and display not their ornaments, except to their husbands or their fathers, or their husbands' fathers, or their sons, or their husbands' sons, or their brothers, or their brothers' sons, or their sisters' sons, or their women, or their slaves, or male domestics who have no natural force, or to children who note not women's nakedness. And let them not strike their feet together, so as to discover their hidden ornaments. And be ye all turned to*

---

[136] Refer to the book: R. Khomeini, *Tahrirolvasyleh*, Iran/Ghom: Darol Elm, 1990.

*God, O ye Believers! that it may be well with you* (Q.24:31).

This Arabic verse of the Qur'an uses the word "foroujahonna" which clearly implies the private and sexual parts of women below the waist. The word "foroujahonna" comes before the word in this verse that is translated as ornaments. Rather than using the exact meaning of the Arabic Qur'anic word within this specific passage, the majority of translations into other languages use much milder words (In English, words such as 'private parts' or 'continence' are used). However, a specific translation of "farj" (the singular of the term "foroujahanna") is used regarding Mary, Jesus' mother, in the Q.21:91 concerning her maidenhood and conception of Jesus.

If the Qur'an teaches women to neglect protecting their private parts from most male relatives and others around them, how is it possible for people to escape sexual immorality? Where in the Christian Scriptures does it teach any woman to show naked and exhibit her private parts to other family members and relatives as is taught in the Qur'an? These types of words and thoughts would be embarrassing and shocking to the least caring inhabitants of many societies, even among those that do not believe in any religion or religious limitations. Isn't immorality among close relatives often exposed in many societies as an abomination? Consider a city or village whose population is only made up of those relatives and other people who are mentioned in the above verse. If women in the streets of that city or village were encouraged to follow the teaching of the Qur'an, how would they be looked upon? What kind of moral messages would the children of the families from that village or city take out to the rest of the world? Wouldn't the boys of that village feel justified in raping their family members or going to rape the women and girls of other villages?

This negligence about protecting the private parts of females has led to big problems amongst some of the families of devoted Muslims. Islamic religious leaders have unavoidably always included instructions in their guide books (Tozih Almasael) about how to handle the circumstances when a man commits adultery with his aunts or has sexual intercourse with a man in his extended family. Khomeini wrote the following;[137]

- If a man before marrying the daughter of his paternal or maternal aunt commits adultery with their mothers, he cannot marry them anymore (subject 2394).

- If after marriage he has not yet had a sexual relationship with his wife (parental or maternal cousin) but has committed adultery with his mother-in-law (aunt), there is no disorder or harm done to their marriage. (subject 2395).

---

[137] Khomeini, R., *Tozih Almasael*, PP.379-80.

- If he commits adultery with a women, he must not marry her daughter, but if he marries a lady, sleeps with her, and then commits adultery with her mother, his wife is still legitimate to him, and also if after marriage yet not having slept with his wife, he commits adultery with his mother in law, it is recommended (not compulsory) to divorce his wife (subject 2396).

- If a man has married the mother or sister or the daughter of another man, and then had a sexual relationship with him, the marriage is still legitimate (subject 2406).

Surely sexual morality should be taught first in the family. How would the Qur'an respond to God's moral example when he took the initiative to clothe Adam and Eve so that their private parts were covered even at a time when they had no children and relatives? Shouldn't parents be a good moral example for their households and for future generations and surrounding people? How could Muslim scholars claim to be morally better than Christians when the contents of the above verse are called shameful by the Bible? How would Muslim scholars and fundamentalists be able to introduce Muhammad to the nations as a perfect moral example, when both young and old know that rape and sexual abuse of women creates insanity and decay in human societies? How could the Qur'an call the Muslim community the best community that has been produced for humankind? Why would it still call Christians and Jews to forgo their most honorable family laws to join the Muslim community that provides the least protection for women?;

> Ye (Muslims) *are the best folk that hath been raised up unto mankind. Ye enjoin the Just, and ye forbid the Evil, and ye believe in God: And if the people of the Book had believed, it had surely been better for them! Believers there are among them, but most of them are perverse* (Q.3:110).

For sure, nominal Muslim men and women would also call the contents of the verse Q.24:31 shameful. The world also would feel sad for the Muslim women who have been degraded in such an immoral way. The world should feel pity for the wives of Muhammad who were called by Muhammad the mothers of Muslim nations. They were left alone or treated carelessly in front of the eyes of their Muslim children. It is obvious that what happened to women in the years of Islam's rise to political power, narrated in the pages of the Qur'an, is nothing other than a reflection of overfed Muslim men's rebellious sexual desires. Even many of the corrupted nations of the world would never publicly accept such a dishonoring attitude against women.

The following are some other examples that the Qur'an records of abuses against women that have been carried on around the world;

- Allah permitted Muhammad to marry the wife of his own adopted son, Zaid, after he caused his adopted son to divorce his wife. The Qur'an clearly states that Muhammad was planning in his heart to have her for himself while she was not yet divorced. However, Allah unveiled the plan for the privilege of his beloved prophet and let the plan be fulfilled (Q.33:37).[138] In the same chapter (sura), the Qur'an insists that Muhammad's companions must not marry his wives and therefore trouble his heart (Q.33:53).

- Allah permitted Muhammad to have any believing woman who gave herself up to him (Q.33:50).[139]

- Muhammad and his wives did not have an honest relationship with each other (Q.66:1-2).[140]

- In selecting his wives, Muhammad's overriding focus was on the outward

---

[138] Also, read: Muhammad-bin Jarir Tabari, *Tarikh-al-rosol val-molouk*, PP.1064-6.
[139] Examples: Ibid., PP.1103,1297-9.
[140] More examples: Ibid. PP.1294-1298.

appearance of girls and ladies rather than a sincere love. He divorced his new wives after having his private time with them and noticing that they were not as young as he expected or seeing stains on their skins (cf. Q.33:52).[141]

- Though Muhammad was over fifty, he preferred to marry very young females. He married a girl, called Ayshah, at the age of six.[142]

- Muslim men were encouraged to possess the enslaved girls and take the enslaved mothers for themselves (Q.4:24; 33:52), ignoring the love and dependency they had towards their children and husbands.

- The judgement of the Qur'an was quiet towards Muslims who forced their female slaves into prostitution in order to gain more money (Q.24:33).

- Men are superior to women and they have the right to beat and leave them alone in their beds if they oppose their husbands' desires (Q.4:34).

---

[141] Ibid., PP.1296-7.
[142] Ibid., PP.930-3,1290-2.

Arabian history proves that respect for pre-Islamic women was greater beyond comparison to the way women were treated in the Islamic era;

> *And abide still in your houses, and go not in public decked as in the day of your former ignorance...* (Q.33:33).

At one time women were highly respected by Arab men. They were called equals and companions. They were treated as people with free choice. No one had the right to regard them as second class, slaves or chattels. Just like men, their creative and influential role was present in all the affairs of life. Certainly in some respects Islam may have raised women to a higher level of civilization but the price for this was a highly decreased level of social influence for women and a lower overall status when comparison is made to the pre-Islamic era.[143]

The Gospel of the Son Jesus Christ is against:

- Women's immodesty before male relatives

- Discrimination against women

- The assertion of superiority of men over women

- The assertion of superiority of non-slaves over slaves

---

[143] Read R. A. Nicholson, PP.87-90.

- The assertion of the superiority of one nation over another

- War and blood-shed against other religions

In contrast, Qur'anic faith and rule have allowed all of these things to happen.

## The Cleansing Power of Jesus' Death

The treatment of women by Islamic leaders can never be reconciled with the values of the kingdom of heaven. The Gospel of Jesus Christ calls such abuses the immorality of fleshly people. Indeed, the core message of Jesus Christ is the freeing of mankind from the immorality of the flesh and the transferring of mankind into the kingdom of heaven. This freedom was provided through the death of Jesus Christ on the Cross. The love of Jesus Christ and his atoning death freed believing men, women, children, slaves and masters from immorality and transformed them into a good moral example for the world no matter what their gender or race;

> Love ... does not delight in evil but rejoices with the truth. It always protects, always trusts, always hopes, always perseveres. Love never fails (1Cor.13:4-8).

In the Gospel all humankind are equally under the power of sin against God and God treats them equally. After any of them are saved from the kingdom of immorality and brought back into the kingdom of morality through the Son Jesus Christ, they are still equal in the eyes of God but this time they are under the power and guidance of His love and grace. In the kingdom of Satan they were not able to be in harmony with each other, because their bodies belonged to sin and immorality. However, now in the kingdom of heaven, their changed lives are no longer used for immorality, but for the will of God (1Cor.6:15-20). They are made harmonious with one another in love and respect. By believing in Christ, His living words are written on the hearts of believing men and women and His words guide their morality in their relationships with each other.

## The Leading Agent of Purification

The Gospel of Jesus Christ, unlike the Qur'an, teaches us that the salvation of a person comes before their moral purification and perfection. A person is not able to represent the goodness of God unless transferred to that first state; that is, saved and reconciled with God. In other words, a person cannot be morally good until saved from evil and born into goodness. According to the Christian Gospel, a person cannot get rid of sexual immorality, impurity and debauchery, idolatry and witchcraft, hatred and discord, jealousy, fits of rage, selfish ambition, drunkenness, orgies, and the like until renewed by God and saved from the corrupted nature. In Christianity, God first changes the status of a person before extending the invitation to act righteously. The person must first be brought into a right situation or state in order to do right. However, in Islam, it is the opposite. A sinful person is asked to be morally good before being enabled to be so.

Muslims are not in paradise yet and they would need to be in order to claim that they are morally better than true Christians. Simply enforcing a religious law by political forces cannot guarantee the moral purity of a person or a society. Political forces are not able to rescue a human's soul from the effect of spiritual evil. An inner change is needed in order to give a person a fresh start leading him/her towards a higher quality of morality. Therefore, moral purification is the consequence of salvation, which is the exodus from the power and effects of evil. God first saves and brings people back to their original state and then asks them to be good and just in their relationship with others. Humankind first must be brought into a righteous position in order to become morally right.

According to the teaching of the Bible, salvation, which is provided only through God, is received on earth and lasts forever. The Qur'an on the contrary, believes that salvation does not take place during life on earth, but in the life after death although a person's fate after death is uncertain. This theological comparison between Islam and Christianity indicates that the Christian faith and not the Muslim faith has the privilege of being the model for good morality on earth. We all know that issues of morality and immorality are the most important issues for life on earth. Immorality started on earth after Adam and Eve sinned against God, and has been a problem ever since. Therefore, immorality must be dealt with during life on earth. Christians believe that God, as the only Saviour must enter the scene and purify men and women, preparing them to act righteously here on earth. God must enter the realm of physical life in order to prepare humankind to be a good example. Humankind must be made good on earth in order to act righteously. This is another major difference between Islam and Christianity. Islam falls short of accepting God's own initiative for renewing the hearts of humankind. Therefore, unlike the Islamic faith, the Christian faith has invited salvation into the arena of the physical world in order to unchain humanity providing them as a good moral example for the world. A spiritually chained man is not able to know the leadership of God and cannot claim that, 'I am a godly man and have a good relationship with others!' He is not able to follow the instructions of God unless he is unchained. The fallen man's first need is to be unchained by God; that is, purified by God. This is what the Bible teaches. This can be said in very simple religious terms. A human heart not purified from inhuman deeds by God, will not be able to have a true relationship with God or neighbor. If a heart has not risen from its fallen state, the impure deeds of that impure heart cannot link to the pure, holy, just, caring and loving God. Purification, salvation and transformation must involve the care, love, justice and holiness of God. This means that God must be at work and in control of this great change;

> *When you were slaves to sin, you were free from the control of righteousness. What benefit did you reap at that time from the things you are now ashamed of? Those things result in death. But now that you have been set free from sin and have become slaves to God, the benefit you reap leads to holiness and the result is eternal life. For the wages of sin is death, but the gift of God is eternal life in Christ Jesus our Lord* (Rom.6:20-22).

We understand that the so-called Christian world has extensively failed to surrender itself to Jesus Christ. Therefore, it is the disbelief in Jesus Christ that has spread immorality among those who apparently live under the name of Christianity. For the Gospel of Jesus Christ, there is only one type of Christian in the world, only those who are saved from the ruler of immorality. Muslims, therefore, must not take the immorality of so-called Christian societies as a sign of the Christian faith having shortcomings. It would be a great help for Muslims in removing their misconceptions, if they would refer to the Gospel of Jesus Christ and compare it with their own religious scriptures. "Jesus Christ came to challenge every culture on the face of the earth so that we might gain a perspective from higher ground."[144]

As a result, no perfect religion allows a person to hurt others for any reason, but rather equips the person to be a blessing to all. The real God is the loving God. The real God provides the way for our hearts and minds to be freed from the bondage to Satan that results in immorality. The resulting renewal is lived out in loving and just relationships.

---

[144] R. Zacharias, P.36.

# SECTION SIX:

# Who Is the Saviour of the Soul, God or Man?

## What does the Qur'an Teach about Salvation?

Does the Qur'an believe in the lostness of humankind? Is salvation a major and serious issue in the Qur'an? Do Muslims content themselves with their own ability to work out salvation as the Qur'an teaches or do they cry to God to save them?

The Qur'anic evidence shows that companionship with Satan diverts mankind from God forever;

> *And whoso shall withdraw from the Warning of the God of Mercy, we will chain a Satan to him, and he will be his fast companion: For the Satan will turn men aside from the Way, who yet shall deem themselves rightly guided; Until when man shall come before us, he shall say, 'O Satan, would that between me and thee were the distance of the East and West.' And a wretched companion is a Satan* (Q.43:36-38).

The Qur'an also teaches that when Adam and Eve were deceived by Satan they were expelled out of Paradise (*Janah*), were made enemies of one another and in this way they were lost;

> *So he* (Satan) *beguiled them* (Adam and Eve) *by deceit: and when they tasted of the tree, their nakedness appeared to them, and they began to sew together upon themselves the*

*leaves of the garden. And their Lord called
to them, 'Did I not say to you, "Verily, Satan
is your declared enemy." ' They said, 'O our
Lord! With ourselves have we dealt
unjustly: if thou forgive us not and have pity
on us, we shall surely be of those who perish.'
He said, 'Get ye down, the one of you an
enemy to the other; ...O children of Adam! let
not Satan bring you into trouble, as he drove
forth your parents from the Garden
(Jannah)...(Q.7:22-24,27).*

Similarly Noah (Q.11:47; 71:27), Abraham (Q.14:41),
Moses (Q.7:151; 26:82; 28:16) and Muhammad
(Q.47:19; 48:2) all call themselves sinners in the
Qur'an and show concern for the result of their own
sins and ask God to forgive them. Only Jesus is
perfect and holy according to the Qur'an (Q.19:18-
19); He is the Word and Spirit of God (Q.4.171b;
19:17); He is the proof of resurrection (Q.43:61); He
is in heaven (Q.4:158) and will come again and
judge the world at the end (c.f. Q.3:55; 4:158).[145]

The Qur'an states that no one except God will be
able to help the sinner;

*Not according to your wishes, or the wishes
of the people of the Book, shall these things
be. He who does evil shall be recompensed*

---

[145] Also read; A. M. A. Shahrestani, *Tozih-almelal,*
P.340.

*for it. Patron or helper, beside of God, shall he find none* (Q.4:123)

How does God help the sinner in order to be saved? Is it through the direct revelation of God or through the human agent?

There are verses in the Qur'an and in the Bible which bring forth the meaning that the descendants of Adam and Eve cannot be trusted because of their sinful nature;

> *Verily, we proposed to the Heavens, and to the Earth, and to the Mountains to receive the Faith, but they refused the burden, and they feared to receive it. Man undertook to bear it, but has proved unjust, senseless* (Q.33:72)!

> *There is no one righteous, not even one* (Rom.3:10).

> *Cursed is the one who trusts in man, who depends on flesh for his strength and whose heart turns away from the LORD* (Jer.17:5).

This is because of the spiritual loss as a result of their rebellious nature against God. Although God calls and chooses some of these earthly and sinful people and uses them to announce His message and plan of salvation, He never abandons the plan of salvation into their hands. He rather undertakes it through His own Word and Spirit (Jesus) who is from heaven. God is pleased when people trust in the One who comes from heaven for salvation rather than in anyone who is from the earth.

Why has God chosen this way? Because the One who is from heaven is God's own Spirit, above all and able to save people. He differs completely in essence from anyone who is from the earth. The one from the earth has inherited the corrupt qualities of Adam and Eve and therefore is lost and in need of a Saviour. The One who has come from heaven is 'the Word and the Spirit' of God, and therefore, can reveal the will, truth and glory of God into a person's life (John1:1-3, 14). That is why Jesus says, 'Anyone who has seen me has seen the Father' (John14:9).

The possibility for people to be saved when they rely on the One who is from heaven is one hundred per cent. Reliance on any one who is from the earth makes salvation impossible. From the Bible and the Qur'an we understand that the essence of Jesus is from heaven and is purely good, but Moses or Muhammad, both descendants of Adam and Eve, are sinful. This is God's logical reason for Jesus being called sinless and trustworthy, while all other prophets are called sinners and incomparable with Jesus. It was these characteristics of Jesus Christ that sealed the prophetic line with His essence and provided such an opportunity that people could come face to face with God rather than only hearing about Him. God provided people with a heavenly opportunity so they could personally put their hands in His hands. How can a man who is the descendant of Adam and Eve, and thereby lost in the sinful world, be trusted for this position of reconciliation? 'They cannot be trusted' is the message of the Bible;

> *He* (Jesus) *is the stone you builders rejected, which has become the capstone. Salvation is found in no one else, for there is no other name under heaven given to men by which we must be saved* (Acts 4:11-12).

The Bible, unlike the Qur'an, introduces God as the One who does not want to leave the problem of sin for the life after. God is zealous to wipe out the problems of sin now. Furthermore, He does not want people to suffer the fault of their parents, Adam and Eve, on earth and into eternity. The problem, which arose in this world, must be dealt and solved in this world. It is here on earth that humankind must be brought back to their original state and enjoy life with God. For this reason, Jesus Christ took responsibility on the Cross for the sins of the world in order to reconcile God and humankind.

We need to be transferred from the dominion of darkness into God's kingdom so we can have an intimate relationship with God and live in harmony with His personality and will. This transformation simply means, 'to be with God and in God, to live and act in God and with God'. How can a rebellious and sinful man, who is lost and dead in the eyes of

God and deserves not to be with Him, be transformed into God's kingdom and enabled to live for God? Who will be the best person to undertake this ministry of transformation; the one who is from earth (sinful man), or the One who is from heaven (the Spirit of God)? Any one who loves justice and holiness will certainly vote for the Spirit who is sinless, and who came down and revealed Himself in Jesus Christ. Therefore, all humankind, including Muslims, need to listen to the cry of their conscience for salvation and allow the Spirit of God, who is from heaven, to remove the barriers in front of them and reconcile them with God.

## Contradictions

As it was stated earlier, the Qur'an does not always hold one particular view about an issue. The Qur'an's ideas about salvation are subject to this instability. Therefore, it is impossible to derive a perfect plan for salvation from the verses of the Qur'an.

The Qur'an encourages its followers to be good and do right so that they might enter heaven after death. Yet it states that everybody, both righteous and unrighteous, will be first led to hell by Allah!;

> *And observe prayer at early morning, at the close of the day, and at the approach of night; for the good deeds drive away the evil deeds...* (Q.11:114).

*Doth not man bear in mind that we made him at first, when he was nought? And I swear by the Lord, we will surely gather together them and Satans: then will we set them on their knees round Hell: Then will we take forth from each band those of them who have been stoutest in rebellion against the God of Mercy: Then shall we know right well to whom its burning is most due: No one is there of you who shall not go down unto it - This is settled decree with thy Lord - Then will we deliver those who had the fear of God, and the wicked will we leave in it on their knees* (Q.19:67-72).

This is contrary to the Gospel of Jesus Christ. God has created a great chasm between hell and heaven as a matter of protection for the righteous (Luke16:26). The Bible teaches that the righteous must be kept safe from the effect of hell forever, from the time of faith placed in the Son, Jesus Christ. For any person who comes to Christ, has eternal life and hell and its sting is swallowed up in victory forever (1Cor.15:53-57). This is the major work of the Son Jesus Christ. Every prophet before Jesus expected Him to enter the world and to undertake this saving act. The New Testament of Christ reveals how this was done, by removing death and its sting from the lives of His believers (Isa.25:8; Rev.20:14-15).

However, despite the above contradictions in the Qur'an, Islam teaches that fallen man is capable of transferring himself to the status mankind held before the fall. It is not for God to save man, but for man to save himself. Though in the Qur'an God has been introduced as a compassionate God, his compassion does not mean, as in Christianity, that he stretches His hand to save the lost. He is called compassionate only because he shows man how to rely on his own good deeds for salvation. In other words, in Islam man is the savior, but in Christianity God is the Saviour.

The disunity that exists among the Qur'an's own verses concerning the issue of salvation, and Muhammad's own words regarding this issue, result in Islam being the most uncertain religion in the world when it comes to the subject of salvation. Even Islamic theologians wonder about how to deal with the conflicting views presented within the Qur'an. They wonder about which ideas to promote; the importance of man's good deeds flowing from the exercise of his free will, or the will of Allah who condemns man for what man cannot help doing?

The Bible, contrary to the Qur'an, teaches that fallen man must first rise from the fallen state. It does not just give a theoretical instruction that leads to uncertainty. Rebellious humankind breaks relationship with God and consequently establishes relationship with Satan. Relationship with God and Satan simultaneously is impossible – a relationship with one means separation from the other. However, it must be taken into consideration that

Satan, unlike God, does not believe in freedom. For this reason, he blinds them to the truth. His plan is to chain his companions in his kingdom forever. The only source that can break this chain is God. Sin results in slavery to sin and to Satan and renders a person weaker than Satan. Self-rescue from the hand of Satan is impossible. But God transfers anyone who asks Him for Salvation into His kingdom (Rom.6:20-23).

The following verses of the Qur'an clearly prove that some of Allah's deeds are not different but complementary to Satan's work with humankind. Allah disables men and women to promote the kingdom of darkness in the same way as Satan. These verses prove that humankind is caught up in the unstable will of Allah that diminishes the will of humans below that of what had been ordained for them in the beginning. He sometimes strengthens Satan, hands over humankind to him, or calls them back to himself;

> *SAY: Nothing can befall us but what God hath destined for us ... (Q.9:51).*

> *...God hath set a seal upon their[146] hearts: they have no knowledge (Q.9:93).*

---

[146] Those who do not believe, stay behind, and do not fight for the cause of Islam.

*What He pleases will God abrogate or confirm: for with Him is the source of revelation* (Q.13:39).

*But will it ye shall not, unless God will it, for God is Knowing, Wise* (Q.76:30).

*Why are ye two parties on the subject of the hypocrites, when God has cast them off for their doings? Desire ye to guide those whom God hath led astray? But for him whom God leadeth astray, thou shalt by no means find a pathway* (Q.4:88 and cf. 35:8; 74:31).

*Many, moreover, of the Djinn and men have we created for Hell. Heart have they with which they understand not, and eyes have they with which they see not, and ears have they with which they hearken not. They are like the brutes: Yea, they go more astray: these are heedless* (Q.7:179).

*Had thy Lord please he would have made mankind of one religion* (community): *but those only to whom thy Lord has granted his mercy will cease to differ. And unto this hath He created them; for the word of thy Lord shall be fulfilled, "I will wholly fill hell with Djinn and men"* (Q.11:118-119).

*...God misleadeth whom He will, and whom He will he guideth: and He is the mighty, the Wise* (Q.14:4).

*Had we* (God) *pleased we had certainly given to every soul its guidance. But true shall be the word which hath gone forth from me - I will surely fill hell with Djinn and men together* (Q.32:13).

*Before them* (infidels) *have we* (God) *set a barrier and behind them a barrier, and we have shrouded them in a veil, so that they shall not see. Alike is it to them if thou warn them or warn them not: they will not believe* (Q.36:9-10).

*Had God pleased, He could have made you one people: but He causeth whom He will to err, and whom He will He guideth: and ye* (all) *shall assuredly be called to account for your doings* (Q.16: 93).

*And whoso shall withdraw from the Warning of the God of Mercy, we will chain a Satan to him, and he will be his fast companion: For the Satan will turn men aside from the Way, who yet shall deem themselves rightly guided; Until when man shall come before us, he shall say, 'O Satan, would that between me and thee were the distance of the East and West.' And a wretched companion is a Satan* (Q.43:36-38).

*So he* (Satan) *beguiled them* (Adam and Eve) *by deceit: and when they tasted of the tree, their nakedness appeared to them, and they began to sew together upon themselves the leaves of the garden. And their Lord called to them, 'Did I not say to you, "Verily, Satan is your declared enemy." ' They said, 'O our Lord! With ourselves have we dealt unjustly: if thou forgive us not and have pity on us, we shall surely be of those who perish.' He said, 'Get ye down, the one of you an enemy to the other; ...O children of Adam! let not Satan bring you into trouble, as he drove forth your parents from the Garden (Jannah)...(Q.7:22-24,27).*

What does right and wrong mean in Islam? Do right and wrong adopt the opposite meanings from time to time? Are right and wrong two independent values through which the two different kingdoms of God and Satan can be distinguished from each other? Or, are they unified in one kingdom working side by side? Is God the one who leads astray as well as the one who guides in the true path? What does the true and straight path mean in the Qur'an's theology; the path which Muslims call Allah to lead them in?;

*Guide Thou us on the straight path (Q.1:6)*

Unfortunately, the Qur'an presents Satan's role in a more straightforward way than Allah's. Satan's goal is only to lead people to be evil, but Allah's goal is to lead people to be both good and evil. Allah on one hand wishes people to go astray and on the other hand asks people to be accountable. If Allah, after all, can disregard humankind's good deeds that he himself has recommended they do, then what are the benefits of doing good deeds!? If Allah bases salvation upon man's good deeds then why is this contradicted at various points in the Qur'an? Why should people be held accountable for the bad deeds which were inspired into them by Allah? What is the use of religion, its rituals, its requirements, etc? But, if man is destined to be active and responsible for his own salvation, why then should he be left uncertain about his salvation, especially when he has tried his best to be victorious prior to his death? The following verses illustrate the uncertainty of Muhammad's own spiritual future;

> SAY: I (Muhammad) *have no control over what may be helpful or hurtful to me, but as God willeth. Had I the knowledge of his secrets, I should revel in the good, and evil should not touch me. But I am only a warner, and an announcer of good tidings to those who believe* (Q.7:188).

> SAY: I (Muhammad) *am no apostle of new doctrines: neither know I what will be done with me or you. Only what is revealed to me do I follow, and I am only charged to warn openly* (Q.46:9).

Why does Allah withdraw himself from the promises he already has given the righteous? Why would Muhammad, who is called the seal of the prophets, the most righteous of all and the best example for all, not be able to believe in salvation for himself? Why does he deliver such a worrying message to his followers? Who is the cause of this unbelief and uncertainty? Is there any benefit in uncertainty, for which Allah has ordained his people? Why would the Qur'an authorise Muhammad to call people to follow in his footsteps, when he is uncertain about his own future? Why would the Qur'an give authority to Muhammad to judge against any one who has failed to obey him and who has failed to give allegiance to him in this life?;

*SAY: If ye* (people) *love God, then follow me* (Muhammad)*: God will love you, and forgive your sins, for God is forgiving, Merciful. SAY: Obey God and the Apostle; but if you turn away, then verily, God loveth not the unbelievers* (Q.3:31).

*As for those who were infidels and turned others aside from the way of God, to them we will add punishment on punishment for their corrupt doings. And one day we will summon up in every people a witness against them from among themselves; and we will bring thee up as witness against these Meccans: for to thee have we sent down the Book which cleareth up everything, a guidance, and mercy, and glad tidings to those who resign themselves to God* (to Muslims) (Q.16:88-89).

How does the spirit of evangelism in these verses match with the uncertainty of the verses Q.7:188; 46:9, as mentioned above? How could the uncertainty in Islam lead to the "glad tidings" expressed in Q.16:89?

Why does the Qur'an call Muslims the best of all humankind, having the ability and power to guide (order) all other people unto righteousness keeping them away from unbelief, when Muslims are put in an uncertain and passive situation by the Qur'an itself?;

*Ye* (Muslims) *are the best folk that had been raised up unto mankind*...(Q.3:110).

Can holiness, justice, righteousness, love, forgiveness and paradise in Islam go with unbelief, confusion and uncertainty? Then how are Muslims able to open a door to help other people while Allah has not yet opened the door to these people? Why would Muslims be interested in waging jihad to force those people Allah has chosen to stay unbelievers in Islam to be otherwise? Why were many people, whom God led astray and prevented from belief in Islam, killed throughout the history of Islam? Who is responsible for this bloodshed? Who is able to administer the true justice between Muslims and non-Muslims? Who is going to gain justice for the non-Muslim who is crying out? How can a court of justice come to convict those who are not the cause of their own unbelief in Islam? Where does justice fit in the call and cause of Allah? We know that even the elegant words in the Qur'an have left these questions unanswered. Islam intends to have the world, but with a confused theology.

It is because of this huge uncertainty by Allah that Muslim scholars are confused on what to say. The 'Risaleh-i-Barkhavi' (tradition) says: 'All other things are passive, Allah alone is active'. Another tradition (hadith) by Al-Bukhari also informs us of Allah denying man's free will, saying: 'Allah created Adam ... brought forth from him a family and said, I have created this family for hell.' Then a man said to the Prophet (Muhammad), 'Of what use will deeds of any kind be?' He said, 'When Allah creates his servant for Paradise, his actions will be deserving for it until he dies - and when Allah creates one for the fire, his actions will be like those of the people of hell till he dies, when he will enter therein'.[147]

Now the problem is this; if part of mankind was made by force to be passive and created for hell, why then should they be called responsible for their own actions? That is why Islamic theologians are not able to understand the real value, if any, of a 'good life'. What does a 'good life' mean and of what use is it?

---

[147] Read, G. Nehls, PP. 21, 25.

Islamic theologians (Ibn-Hazm for example) ponder the elegant and beautiful words such as holiness, justice, righteousness, love, forgiveness, etc., mentioned in the Qur'an. They say that these words cannot be used theologically and they are unable to understand their real meaning and cannot explain why they are in the Qur'an. They have to use these words in their daily talks, not because they are relevant to and useful in their lives, but because these words are in the Qur'an and cannot be taken out.[148]

God is the only accountable and trustful source of knowledge for humankind. He cannot be the cause of confusion. Confusion in a religion is not anything other than the interference of humankind in God's business. Adam and Eve breached the values of the path that leads to life with God and thus became confused in the dominion of Satan. It was God who saved them and brought them to their original state out of the confusion that they themselves had caused. Confusion arises in our life when we make ourselves dependent on our own theology leading to a state of godlessness. In other words, confusion has no place when someone is with God and He with them. The confusion in Islam is because it has omitted God in its efforts to transfer people from the land of confusion into which they have fallen, back to their original state before sin. Islam has represented God as being totally indifferent about providing an opportunity, through which people

---

[148] Ibid, P. 28.

could become certain of their salvation in this world before death. There is not any basis of assurance for salvation in Islam. Indeed, it is in the certainty of salvation that one discovers the real meaning of each word that comes out of the mouth of almighty God. In other words, those who are in the kingdom of God can understand the real meaning of every word that comes from God. They are able to distinguish between the words that belong to God and the words that do not belong to God. The Lord of salvation saves and enables people to understand his words. The salvation God has brought to people is the salvation that makes the Words of God understandable (1Cor.2:9-13).

In Christianity God saves people and brings them back to himself during the life on earth. Salvation is man's main need and Jesus Christ is the One who has met it fully. That is why Jesus Christ, the Son, is called the Lord of Salvation (Acts 4: 12) and his Gospel is the power of God for the salvation of everyone who believes (Rom.1:16). The Gospel of Christ says, *'if all have sinned and fall short of the glory of God, then all are justified freely by his grace through the redemption that came by Christ Jesus'* (Rom.3: 23-24). Why? The just, holy and kind God reaches out to rescue humankind whom He has created for Himself, giving them the certainty of eternal life in this world for the world to come. With a holy God, this can only be achieved through love and justice.

How?

God created Adam and Eve good and for himself. Satan caused them to sin and to fall far from God. God revealed in His triunity, says to a sinner: 'O sinner, I am love (the Father who desires you be purified and brought back home). I am just (the Son who destroys the source of what is unjust to deliver you from the dominion of darkness into the light) and I am holy (the Spirit who teaches you and convicts you of sin). The **love** of God took the initiative to bring them back (John 3: 16). His **justice** entered the world to rescue them from the dominion of darkness and to bring them back home to be with their Creator and God (Col.1: 13; Romans 5: 1). His **holiness (the Holy Spirit)** also seals and guarantees their inheritance for the day of redemption (Eph.1: 14; 4: 30).

In contrast Allah in the Qur'an has been introduced to the people as the giver of both good and evil. He himself has corrupted Satan so that he can corrupt man;

> *He* (Satan) *said, 'Now, for that thou* (God) *hast caused me to err, surely in thy straight path will I lay wait for them* (humankind)*: Then will I surely come upon them from before, and from their left, and thou shalt not find the greater part of them to be thankful.' He said, 'Go forth from it, a scorned, a banished one! Whoever of them shall follow thee, I will surely fill hell with you, one and all* (Q.7:16-18).

Also, Allah himself has inspired (breathed) the sin into man's soul to make him vulnerable so that he falls into the dominion of Satan;

> By a Soul and Him who balanced it, And (God) breathed into it its wickedness[149] and its piety, Blessed now is he who hath kept it pure (Q.91:7-9).

As is obvious from the verses above, Allah himself has directly tainted the human soul with sin and indirectly, through the devil, has surrounded humankind at all points, making them unable to exit from this corruption. This is not the end of the story. These unfortunate men and women, who were handed over and chained in the impure kingdom of debauchery, are now called to keep their soul pure and free of debauchery; an impossible, unattainable task.

We learn from Sahih Muslim (PP. 1396-1398) that in a dispute between Adam and Moses (!), Moses says: 'you are our father, you did us harm and you caused us to be thrown out of Paradise.' Adam said to him... 'You blame me for an act which Allah had ordained for me 40 years before he created me.' Allah's Apostle then said: 'This is how Adam came to have the better of Moses' (cf. Q.57: 22). We also learn from Abu Huraira's reporting, which Sahih Muslim also confirms, that Muhammad said: 'There

---

[149] The word in Arabic is "fojooraha" which means debauchery.

would be no escape from adultery. Allah has fixed the very portion of adultery which a man will indulge in, and which he of necessity must commit.[150]

Narrated Abu Ayyub Anasari: Abu Salimah reported that when the time of death of Abu Ayyub drew near, he said: I used to conceal from you a thing which I heard from Allah's Apostle (peace be upon him) and I heard Allah's Apostle (peace be upon him) as saying: Had you not committed sins, Allah would have brought into existence a creation that would have committed sin (and Allah) would have forgiven them.[151]

Narrated Abu Hurairah: Allah's Apostle (peace be upon him) said: By Him in whose Hand is my life, if you were not to commit sin, Allah would sweep you out of existence and He would replace (you by) those people who would commit sin and seek forgiveness from Allah, and He would have pardoned them.[152] Abu Hurairah narrated again that Muhammad said, "No child is born but that Satan touches it when it is born whereupon it starts crying loudly because of being touched by Satan, except Mary and her Son"[153].

---

[150] G. Nehls, P.22.
[151] Sahih Al-Musim *Hadith* No.1277
[152] Sahih Al-Musim *Hadith* No.1278
[153] Dr. Muhammad Muhsin Khan, *Sahih Bukhari Vol.6, Hadith 71*, Published by Islamic University, Al Medina Al Munauwara, P.54, ND.

Why did Allah tell Adam and Eve that they shouldn't approach the evil tree when he had already himself inspired this evil desire in their hearts? All the evidence in Islamic writings proves that the Evil Spirit is active in everybody's life before birth, at the time of birth and after birth. This is contrary to the everyday faith of most Muslims as they believe that sin was not inherited through Adam and Eve to all humankind but that sin only comes through a personal relationship with Satan. The writings of Islam imply that a relationship is developed with Evil even before birth by the will of Allah. They consider the Satanic relationship is not only a matter of personal relationship after birth. It goes back even before conception. Therefore when the Qur'an states that Adam and Eve sinned and they were expelled "out of paradise", it was because Allah willed it. As a result, Adam's descendants were born in a place separated from God - the dominion of darkness and this was caused by Allah. It was not Adam's fault, because Allah had ordained sin to Adam before he was created. Sin is ordained by Allah as Muhammad stated in the above narrative and sin harmed Adam and harmed Adam's descendants, through all ages, including Moses.

Allah causes the fall and he then calls upon the people, who are in the dominion of darkness, to follow the truth!! This seems very shocking!! What kind of motivating factors can be found in the dominion of Satan, which can motivate the people to follow the truth? What kind of truth can be found in the kingdom of Satan through which people could fulfill the will of holy God (cf. Q.62:1)? Do pure truth and holiness come out from the assemblies of evil? Or, is it again a combination of good and evil that Islam calls good? How could Islam's theologians derive a pure paradise for the Muslims out of the paradoxes of the Qur'an and the Hadiths? How could this paradise be a place far from the dualism of good and evil and therefore a place of peace and rest forever? How can Muslims wait upon the grace of Allah who has been the giver of both good and evil? How can Muslims call for the so-called grace of Allah who, from the beginning, chose not to have them with himself but with Satan? What good is the Muslims' plea when Allah can, if he wills, cast all, both righteous (!) and unrighteous, into hell? Is hell also for the righteous?

## Blameless God

I personally warm so much to the Lord of the holy Bible that calls to men and women, and says, '*Come now, let us reason together*' (Isa.1: 18). '*Let us see who is right.*' God does not want people to follow Him blindly (John 8: 32). He has created man and woman in his likeness with free will, and enabled them to test and choose freely. Every one, to the level of their God given capacity, must comprehend the goodness of God (Romans 8: 20). If some one, for any reason, tries to veil or ignore their ability to recognize God, they will not be able to hear God. The Qur'an itself describes the difference between

Allah and idols, convincing people to follow Muhammad (Q.7:191-196). It contrasts hell with paradise to convince its followers to walk along with Muhammad. In these instances, it invites people to think and explore!

Muslims need to search and see that God is blameless, and that He never leads his creatures to hell. Muslims must discover the true God who is described as the source and giver of all good. They have to call upon the true God who is purely good and has no evil desires. I can say with pure certainty that, if any Muslim truly desires and is prepared to search for the true God, no matter what the cost, they will find Jesus Christ. Contrary to all the religions of the world, the theology of Jesus Christ has not been founded upon the combination of " good and evil ", but only upon pure good. In the true theology of God, the combination of " good and evil " is dangerous for life (Gen.3: 22-24). One who practices good and evil cannot have fellowship with God, and God can never countenance the friendship of good and evil (Isa.1: 11-16).

In conclusion, which man does God enable to gain salvation? Is it the man who relies on Almighty God who is the only source and giver of all good? Or is it the man who relies on the god that is known as the giver of both good and evil, who positions and chains man in an impossible situation from which to gain salvation? There is a grave distinction between the God who is the giver of all good and the god who is the giver of both good and evil. Anyone, who comes to discover this difference between Christianity and Islam, would eagerly follow the foot steps of Jesus Christ, the Son, who is the only source and giver of all good. Those who desire to relate themselves to the Holy God, must relate themselves first to Jesus Christ. Having realized this definite opportunity, Muslims also, like all the nations of the world, are invited to put their trust in Him who is called the Son of God (Acts 10: 34-36). His nature is far from the mixture of good and evil. He is the first and last when it comes to goodness. The inherent goodness in Him has made him the Master and the Lord of eternal life. He is in heaven and is able to draw people to heaven. Therefore, He is worthy to lead people to eternal life. He is good, the source of good, he does good, he makes all good and he therefore deserves to be the judge between good and evil. Muslims, like all other nations, do desperately need him!

## Sinners, Oppressors and Losers

The effect of sin is beyond all imagination. It has damaged humankind and all people are in desperate need of salvation from God. That is why the pressure from sin in his life caused Muhammad to give up his trust in his good deeds and brought him concern about his uncertain future;

> ...neither know I what will be done with me or you...(Q.46:9)

Satan is openly an enemy of humankind. His job is to lead humankind out of the presence of God through temptation. Anyone who sins becomes a certain loser. There is no one immune from Satanic temptations and sins. This leads to the conclusion that every one has joined the category of people who have lost eternal life. In both the Qur'an and Islamic traditions, it is recorded that Muhammad too was tempted by Satan and sinned against God and humankind. There are many verses in the Qur'an which indicate that all humankind, including prophets, are sinners, oppressors, and losers;

> *Verily, man's lot is cast amid destruction* (Q.103:2).

> *...Man...has proved unjust, senseless* (Q.33:72).

That is why Muslims, including Muhammad, call upon God to guide them into the true way, but not into the way of those who are lost;

> *Guide Thou us on the straight path, the path of those to whom you hast been gracious; - with whom thou are not angry, and who go not astray*[154] (Q.1:6-7).

Muslims recite these verses in their prayers five times a day, asking God to have compassion on them and to rescue them from eternal death. They

---

[154] 'Zaallin' in Arabic, which equals misled, lost, wandered and those who went astray.

are not sure whether they will be losers or winners. Therefore, the issue of 'lostness' is not only with every Muslim according to the Qur'an and Islamic traditions, but is also a serious problem for daily life. Even the most encouraging verses of the Qur'an, which promise future glory (Jannah), prove that all humankind has fallen short of that glory, and is separated from the nature of that eternal life that Muslims long for on earth. The Qur'an calls upon all Muslims and humankind, who have turned away from the presence of God and have lost their place in Paradise (Heaven), to beg to God for the forgiveness of their sins.

Sin has driven eternal life away from humankind. Following this loss, God wants humankind to come back to him. The human heart also longs to reach Him. The whole philosophy of human salvation is centered on how one can return to that original state of assurance of eternal life with God. This is where irreconcilable differences arise between the Qur'an and the Bible. Neither Islam nor any other religion has a clear message about salvation for humankind. All, except Christianity, have left humankind in uncertainty. According to the Bible, this eternal life is based on the grace of the One God who stretches out His hand and saves all who believe in Christ, from the bondage of sin and Satan (Eph.2:8-10). He is the God of Love. He knows that humankind needs a Saviour. He knows that sin has brought humankind into a situation of bondage. Sin has dominated the life of humankind. It is not for men and women to direct their steps any more

(Jeremiah 10:23). They are not able to save themselves from the dominion of sin. Solomon says, *"Who can say, "I have kept my heart pure; I am clean and without sin"* (Proverb 20:9). Job asks, *"Do you have an arm like God's, and can your voice thunder like his?...(if you have and can)...Then I myself will admit to you that your own right hand can save you"* (Job 40:9-14). The power of sin and Satan is beyond the power of humankind. For this reason, we need God to enter the scene of human life in order to save us from the power of sin and Satan.

## No One Is Able to Prevail

Muslims do not realize that no one is able to prevail through their own strength. They are all unconsciously obeying a falsehood and are suffering in many ways. Their attempts to reach God do not have a place in God's plan of salvation. Salvation is the exodus from the dominion of Satan to the kingdom of God. Although the human heart desires for such a release, the corrupt soul **acts** as an obstacle preventing access to the path to freedom. There is a conflict in the soul of humankind between accepting grace and continuing in corruption. There is a conflict in the soul of humankind between the law of God in which humankind delights and to which he or she wants to conform, and the law of sin, which is also appealing. The law of sin captivates and compels us to do that which we do not want to do.[155] Corrupt tendencies in the heart of all humankind preclude them from appearing without any sin in the presence of God. The way to salvation is therefore unattainable by man.

It is obvious that Muslims, like many other nations of the world, love God and try hard to reach him so that their distance from God might be abolished. Although the mainstream culture in Islamic societies says that 'God is with us', the writings of the Qur'an prove to us that God and Muslims are not able to be with each other during the life on earth. If they are with God, they would be in the kingdom of God (paradise) and would not have any need for the daily rituals and practices in order to store up righteousness for the day of judgement. There is a distance between Muslims and God that causes them to try hard to do what is right in this life in order to join God after life. Although the ultimate entry into paradise is not certain, it is theoretically sure to take place after life for those Muslims who meet certain criteria.

The Bible teaches that humankind's choices have brought separation from God (out of the Garden of Eden or out of the kingdom of heaven). This has been the case since Adam and Eve sinned against God, when their hearts and minds were contaminated with everything against God. That is why humankind cannot work salvation for itself. Human philosophy does not lead to God. It may be

---

[155] Iskandar Jadeed, P.4. & cf. Rom.7:18-23.

able to discover the reality of God's existence, but it is not able to lead people to God. That is why the Bible says:

> 'Cursed is the one who trusts in man, who depends on flesh for his strength and whose heart turns away from the Lord. He will be like a bush in the wastelands; he will not see prosperity when it comes. He will dwell in the parched places of the desert, in a salt land where no one lives. But blessed is the man who trusts in the Lord, whose confidence is in him. He will be like a tree planted by the water that sends out its roots by the stream. It does not fear when heat comes; its leaves are always green. It has no worries in a year of drought and never fails to bear fruit' (Jer.17:5-8).

We know that any one who is pure and good deserves to be in heaven (paradise), but the one who has the mixture of good and bad cannot be in heaven. Adam and Eve were good and could therefore stay in the Garden of Eden. However, when they fell into dualism, they were expelled out of the land of trust, Eden. God Himself did not trust them any more; otherwise, he would not have expelled them from the Garden. Adam and Eve could never be trusted on the earth, because they were rebels against God. They committed evil acts and hence, were banished from the land of trust. With their actions, they were not able to satisfy a holy and good God anymore. They could not even be a standard for their Children. Yes, they could be God's messengers on the earth and they could tell themselves and their children about their own wrong doings and they could talk about the standards of God's kingdom. However, they were not able to meet God's standards and couldn't represent it by their lives any more. Only the One that is in and from heaven (Jesus) can be and represent the standard. This is the theology of Jesus Christ, which overcomes human philosophy and logic and therefore makes God known to people and leads many to believe in Him.

There is also some evidence from the practice of the religious lives of Muslims, which proves that salvation cannot be gained by man's deeds. Here are some examples of these evidences that B. Dennett mentions in his book:

- A seeking after God's pardon and forgiveness.

- A longing for assurance of going to heaven.

- A fear of death and the judgement of God.

- Apprehension about Satan's power over them, and their own bent toward evil.

- Bondage to evil spirits, occult practices, and defilement.

- Often they lack any sense of God's loving care, of purpose in life, or that he will answer their requests.[156]

All the evidence proves that **humankind cannot be saved by its own deeds**. Sin has corrupted every one, and no one can make their own way to God. There is no hope for the one who is a sinner, unless he or she accepts God's **perfect plan** for salvation.

Therefore, eternal life is the major issue that needs to be thought about in life and humankind needs to immediately search for and find the true way to it. For this reason, Muslims need to realize the need for personal investigation and discovery of the real foundation for eternal life. It is vital that they read the Bible and see that its words are all about the immediate provision of eternal life for fallen humankind. Muslims must not be put off by the absence of Muhammad's name in the Bible. For the Bible the vital issue is the eternal life that has been provided for the world through Jesus Christ (Luke 2:31; John 3:16; 5:24; 1John 5:13).

---

[156] B. Dennett, *Sharing God's Love with Muslims,* Sth. Holland: The Bible League, 1992, PP.11-12.

# SECTION SEVEN:

# How Can Muslims Follow the Son?

# Through the Active Word
# and Love of the Son

The Apostle Paul said, 'the Gospel is the power of God' (Rom.1:16). He also said that the proclamation of the word of Christ delivered him from the Lion's mouth (2Tim.4:17). He wrote this because he experienced the power of the Gospel in every event of his ministry from the time he came to faith in Christ to the end. There was not a single experience in his ministry that disillusioned him about being a spokesman for Christ. The active word, love and humility of Christ in him humbled his enemies at the feet of Christ, just as had happened to him. We read in the Gospel that even a jailer washed the wounds that the chains had left on Paul's body (Acts16:33).

Those who have tasted the pain of being in a bitter and harsh jail know the severity of a harsh jailer. In situations like these, a jailer is appointed to this position in order to give prisoners as much emotional and physical pain and persecution as possible. He has to be a person who enjoys the pain of his prisoners. He must be able to dig into the already existing wounds on the prisoner's body in order to increase the pain to an even higher level. He tortures, rapes, kills and does everything that might help to change the prisoner's mindset. When a jailer such as this humbles himself and comes to follow the faith of his humiliated prisoner, there must be a loving and changing power in the message of that prisoner. This effect on jailers is what Christian prisoners have been seeing in the prisons of various countries ever since the rise of Christianity.

There is indeed power in the loving message of Jesus Christ that even amazes the most brutal people and causes them to change their mindset. The history of Christianity has recorded amazing testimonies of how the enemies of Christ turned and became his friends and followers. Paul's life is evidence of this. He had a strong hatred towards Christians. This led him to be a violent persecutor of the followers of Christ. The following is Paul's account of the actions he committed against Christians;

> *On the authority of the chief priests I put many of the saints in prison, and when they were put to death, I cast my vote against them. Many a time I went from one synagogue to another to have them punished, and I tried to force them to blaspheme. In my obsession against them, I even went to foreign cities to persecute them* (Acts 26:10-11).

After his encounter with Christ, there was a dramatic change in his attitude towards Christians. Where he once had a burning desire to eliminate them, he now had a genuine concern for their well being despite all the hardships he faced as a result,

*I have worked much harder, been in prison more frequently, been flogged more severely, and been exposed to death again and again. Five times I received from the Jews the forty lashes minus one. Three times I was beaten with rods, once I was stoned, three times I was shipwrecked, I spent a night and a day in the open sea, I have been constantly on the move. I have been in danger from rivers, in danger from bandits, in danger from my own countrymen, in danger from Gentiles; in danger in the city, in danger in the country, in danger at sea; and in danger from false brothers. I have labored and toiled and have often gone without sleep; I have known hunger and thirst and have often gone without food; I have been cold and naked. Besides everything else, I face daily the pressure of my concern for all the churches* (2Cor.11:23-28).

So, what caused Paul to cease his continuous massacre of Christians and then to turn and become a loving and compassionate follower of Christ who had a concern for all churches? Paul himself has answered this question by saying that 'the gospel is the power of God' (Rom.1:16). If there was no power in Christ's words, He could not possibly send us empty handed to all the nations of the world;

"All authority in heaven and on earth has been given to me. Therefore go and make disciples of all nations, baptizing them in the

285

name of Father, and of the Son and of the Holy Spirit, and teaching them to obey everything I have commanded you. And surely I am with you always, to the end of the age" (Matt.28:18-20).

Those who have experienced the power of His word and love know that nothing can separate them from the love of Christ and His love for the nations. Paul quotes this in a similar way;

> For I am convinced that neither death nor life, neither angels nor demons, neither the present nor the future, nor any powers, neither height nor depth, nor anything else in all creation, will be able to separate us from the love of God that is in Christ Jesus our Lord (Rom.8:38-39).

Human history would never have been able to produce such a testimony without the powerful work of Christ, that despite all trials and tribulations you never want to turn aside from proclaiming His loving message;

> For God so loved the world that he gave his one and only Son, that whoever believes in him shall not perish but have eternal life. For God did not send his Son into the world to condemn the world, but to save the world through him (John3:16-17).

We have to keep in mind that Jesus Christ is the Lord of all nations, including Muslims, and all power and authority in heaven and earth belong to Him. Muslims like all other people groups of the world need to be brought to a position where they can bring glory and praises to Christ. In order for this to be fulfilled, they need to understand who the true God is and how He has revealed Himself to humankind.

The way that Christians minister to Muslims is quite different to the way Muslims relate to others. Unlike Muslims, we do not believe in 'jihad' that causes domination, repression and war. We believe in showing the 'unconditional love' of Christ. The words of Jesus Christ indicate that war against flesh and blood and breaching people's freedom and dominating their lives reflects the worst motives of selfishness and greed (James4:1-3). We do have a war but the Bible makes it clear that it is not against flesh and blood but against Satan. Our weapons are quite different to those that the nature of Islam requires Muslims to use. The 'weapons' of our war are motivated by 'love, joy, peace, patience, kindness, goodness, faithfulness, gentleness, and self-control' (Gal.5:22). Only these divine tools can be used to carry out the Christian ministry. Those who want to fight Satan must use these weapons in all their relationships with others. There are many good reasons for Christians to use these tools for evangelism;

- The word of our Lord Jesus Christ is living and active, sharper than any sword. It is addressed to people's conscience (2Cor.4:2) and therefore penetrates minds and hearts and changes them (Heb.4:12).

- We want to win the hearts of people for the Almighty God. Can force be used to win people's hearts? No. No one's heart is satisfied with force and violence but by love. Force is for those who do not have confidence to explore other ideas and who do not compare their religion with others.

- Jesus said, 'My kingdom is not of this world. If it were, my servants would fight' (John18:36).

- We love all the nations of the world, and want to lead them to God.

- Our ministry is for the Kingdom of heaven that has been already established victoriously through the blood of the Son Jesus Christ who reconciled the world to God. We are the children of this Kingdom, we have victory over Satan, and are therefore at peace in this world. We cannot prescribe anything other than 'love and peace'.

## Through the Messengers of the Son

How can Muslims believe in the One of whom they have not heard? And how can they hear without someone preaching to them (Rom.10:14)? Christians have an obligation to proclaim the Gospel;

> *Yet when I preach the Gospel, I cannot boast, for I am compelled to preach. Woe to me if I do not preach the Gospel!* (1Cor.9:16).

God has made it possible for Christians to reach out to other nations. He has left some positive aspects remaining in every culture in order to make our preaching understandable and convincing. Jesus delivered his message in the same way. He used the values of Jewish culture in His parables so that they could understand and relate the parables to their lives. In a similar way, Christians too can use the different aspects of the various Muslim cultures in order to make their messages understandable. Some of these cultural aspects that can be used are the following;

- Muslims do know that God can save, but they do not know that God can save them now. Neither do they know that God has paid the price for their salvation and has prepared the way through Christ, for them to come back to Him (Rom.5: 18-19).

- Muslims are sure that God is Almighty, omnipresent and He controls everything now and forever, but they do not know that God is also able to give them assurance of salvation now.

- They do know that God is the source of all life but are unaware that God has set before them the choice of life or death, blessings or curses during their life on earth.

- In theory, Muslims agree that God can reveal Himself and make Himself known to man in any possible way. However, they neither believe nor accept that God became flesh, and made Himself known as the Son of Man in order to seek and save the lost of the world.

- Ironically, Muslims do not know some of the characteristics which are mentioned about Jesus in the Qur'an itself. If they would take a moment and compare the Jesus of the Qur'an with Muhammad they would be shocked and amazed by the supremacy of Jesus.

- Muslims do not know that the prophets they honour have said that Jesus is more than a prophet; He is the Almighty God, He will reign forever.

- All Muslim cultures believe that God must be given first priority. This could help Christians to convince them to open up their minds to learn about God.

- Religion in Islamic language means 'the way'. Muslims need to be awakened to the fact that to discover 'the way' involves searching with an open mind and open eyes. Wholeheartedness is the key success factor in Christ's theology (Jn.8:32-33; Acts17:23-27). It is the theology of wholeheartedness that has made the Bible the power of God for every one who believes (Isa.1:18; 2Tim.1:12b; Rom.1:16).

  *God did this so that men would seek him and perhaps reach out for him and find him....... (Acts 17:27a).*

- Muslims have not been encouraged to know their own religious Scriptures. In fact, one of the major obstacles that makes it so hard for Muslims to understand the Christian faith is their lack of ability to compare the Qur'an to the Bible.

# Evangelism Is Possible among Muslims

We can do everything through Christ who gives us strength (Phil.4: 13). Whatever we ask in His name, he will do it and we will receive the courage and joy to follow him (John 16: 24).
Christian evangelism is banned in almost all Islamic countries. The degree of severity of punishment varies from one country to another. However, this religious intolerance has caused Christian missionaries to consider evangelism among Muslims too difficult. This has left Muslims with little exposure to the Gospel.

Christians have to realize the purpose of Jesus' call; *"Come follow me and I will make you fishers of men."* (Matt.4:19). God loves Muslims no matter how harsh or strong their beliefs are and He takes no pleasure even in the death of the wicked (Ezek.33:11). He wants everyone, including Muslims, to come to Him (2 Pet.3: 9). For this reason, God has chosen the church of Jesus Christ as 'His primary instrument of revelation on earth'[157], to proclaim His salvation to the world;

*Through the church, the manifold wisdom of God should be made known...*(Eph.3:10).

---

[157] G. Otis, JR., *The Last of the Giants,* USA: Chosen Books, 1993, P.34.

Despite all sorts of pain and even death threats (2 Cor.11: 23-33), Jesus sent Paul to preach the Gospel of salvation to all, including His enemies. When Jesus and His followers show compassion towards their enemies, this does not make sense according to the world's logic and philosophy. One must enter into the mindset of Jesus in order to be able to understand His always forgiving and servant attitude towards His enemies. For Jesus, the hardest heart needs to come face to face with the most powerful and amazing love that stands firm and never changes. What could possibly have motivated Paul to continue his ministry despite so many unbearable calamities that occurred? The world would answer 'madness' whereas Christians point to the 'amazing love and grace' of Jesus. Paul says, *'my dear brothers stand firm. Let nothing move you. Always give yourselves fully to the work of the Lord, because you know that your labor in the Lord is not in vain* (1Cor.15:58).

There are two benefits to be gained in evangelizing those who are most antagonistic to the Gospel. Firstly, Christians understand and realize the full power of the Gospel as they see results. And secondly, to open the eyes of even the most closed people and to turn them from darkness to light; from the power of Satan to Christ - so that they may receive forgiveness of sins and a place among those who are sanctified by faith in Christ (Acts 26:17-19).

Every Muslim, from childhood, has heard that Islam supersedes every other religion in the world. Many

Muslims wish that Christians would realize the superiority of Islam and become converts. Likewise, Christians also expect a similar response from Muslims. If people are able to dialogue in a non threatening way and as equals in a friendly environment, then it will be much easier to know whether Christianity or Islam is true. More often than not, it has been hard to find such a friendly situation in Islamic countries. Many Islamic people live in fear of the fundamentalist authorities. Islam's strong reliance on the power of the sword for victory has marginalised the freedom of speech and open discussion within Islamic societies. The spirit of Islam is in control of every Muslim, and has taught and armed them to reject or to attack anything other than Islam. It is so difficult for a person who is armed physically or mentally against the truth, to understand the truth. It is impossible to understand the truth without physical and mental disarmament and there must be continual reference to mutual respect and love.

Christians will not be able to reach Muslims in any other way except through the way given to us of the Cross. In order to bring Muslims to the foot of the Cross, Christians continually need to meditate on and live out the lessons that Jesus taught during his three years of ministry on earth. At the end of Christ's journey on earth, a military man, who was watching the agony of Jesus on the Cross, said, *'Surely this man was the Son of God'* (Mark15:39). The unceasing love of Christ created such a full-hearted confession from the life of an armed enemy.

The love of Christ can also bring Muslims to such a confession.

Christians need to build strong friendships with Muslims based on confidence, love, and honesty. Confidence is the unshakeable base for Christian evangelism. Love and honesty are both powerful tools for building trusting relationships. They also help to create active listeners. Love and honesty will also help Christians to show themselves as genuine seekers through their willingness to study other faiths and creeds. Any ministry approach that attempts to reach Muslims that is not based on an open sharing of knowledge and understanding cannot be a real Christian ministry and thus becomes a threat to real ministry. For this reason, Christians need to invest time in building friendships with Muslims, and they need to grow in their understanding of the cultural aspects of the people they are getting to know. In Islamic societies, friendship is extremely important. Friendship leads Muslims to listen to you. This is one of the reasons why some Islamic countries feel threatened by such friendships and forbid Muslims to be friends with Christians.

Muslims need to discover and know whether the Bible or the Qur'an is the Word of God. They need to know which one introduces the real justice of God. They need to ask which one truly cares for the world and provides salvation for humankind? Muslims need to be assured that Jesus can answer their desperate need for salvation and can erase any uncertainty about salvation in their lives. We can prove to them how we now have assurance of salvation in Him. We can help Muslims by using simple illustrations - such as the parable of the lost sheep. This parable for example tells that there is no chance of salvation for the lost in the den of wolves (Satan) unless someone, who is the source of all good, stretches out his hand and saves the lost. Sin not only has made man like a lost sheep but has also wounded and disabled him so that he has no power to reach salvation. You cannot be saved until the shepherd (Lord) of salvation comes to save you. That is why, in Christianity, unlike other religions, God seeks man and saves him (Luke 19: 10).

The verses of the Qur'an prove that when Adam and Eve sinned, they lost their glorious life in paradise and were sent to the land of sin, hatred and humiliation. There was not any hope for them to be saved from the hands of Satan. The only thing they immediately realized and acted upon, was to call upon God for salvation;

> *They* (Adam and Eve) *said, 'O our Lord! With ourselves have we dealt unjustly: if thou forgive us not and have pity on us, we shall surely be of those who perish* (Q.7:23).

This verse clearly declares that salvation depends on God's forgiveness and not on man's deeds. This could be one of the reasons why the Qur'an in another section states that all humankind is in a complete state of loss;

*I swear by the declining day! Verily, man's lot is cast amid destruction* (Q.103:1-2).

These verses point to the fact that men and women live in a land which is far from the glory of paradise, where Satan lives and is active. As a result, all live in and with sin.

We can assist Muslims by helping them to comprehend God's reason for expelling Adam and Eve from their residing place, paradise (Eden). God could not bear the companionship of Adam and Eve any more. They had trusted Satan, had sinned and placed themselves in a situation opposed to God's holiness, thereby falling short of the glory of God. The holiness of God separates Him from all those who are not holy. The holiness of God requires that everyone who desires to have a relationship with God must conform to His standard. The holiness of God requires a faith that gives absolute priority to the plan and will of God. Adam and Eve lost their place in God's presence, because they changed allegiance and became chained to the plan of Satan, and in this way lost communion with God.

How then, given that Adam and Eve fell into the realm and dominion of unrighteous Satan, could they become righteous once again and thereby fit for the kingdom of God?

Which righteousness, the righteousness of the world or the righteousness of heaven, is the real righteousness that can lead us to our original position with God?

We can help Muslims to understand that the true God does not base His plan of salvation upon the deeds of those who are in the dominion of sin. We can help them to question their consciences about how it is possible that God can require good deeds considering they are not released from the dominion of Satan. In their inner beings, people long for God, and for this reason, they try their best to please Him. But the problem is that they are not yet released from the bondage of Satan and therefore, they cannot please God. Every "good" deed performed by one who is in the realm of Satan, is contaminated by the character of Satan. A person can only perform deeds pleasing to God when they allow God to release them from Satan and bring them into a righteous position; in other words, into the kingdom of good (heaven).

God knows that no one, not even a great prophet (Ezek.14: 20) can find salvation by his own strength or save other lives by his own strength - because all were born in sin. That is why God decided from the beginning to take the initiative Himself to save this otherwise hopeless world.

He revealed Himself in Christ and dwelt among us to save the world. All the prophets in the Bible were sent to preach this glorious coming and revelation of God among the people (Ex.29:44-45; Lev.26:11-12; Ps.96:10-13; Isa.7:14; 9:6-7; 40:3-5; Eze.37:26-27; Mal.3:1; John1:1-3,14; 14:9). They were sent to prepare the world to welcome God's

Divine intervention, His act of salvation for the world. If a man rejects divine aid, he will never experience salvation. Therefore, it is wise not to waste this great opportunity, but to come now and hear God's amazing reasoning about salvation. He says, *"Come now, let us reason together. Though your sins are like scarlet, they shall be as white as snow; though they are red as crimson, they shall be like wool"* (Isa.1: 18). *"Sin is crouching at your door; it desires to have you, but you must master it"* (Gen.4: 7) through Christ who is able to forgive sins (Luke5:20).

# Bibliography

Andrae, T., *Muhammad: The Man and His Faith,* New York: Harper & Row Publishers, 1955.

Anderson, M. N., *Proud to be a Muslim,* California, 1993.

Anderson, N., *The World's Religions,* England: Inter Varsity Press, 1994.

Armajani, Y., *Middle East Past and Present,* Prentice-Hall, 1970.

Armstrong, K., *A History of God,* London: Heinemann Pub., 1993.

Ayyubi, M., (ed), *Khumeini Speaks Revelation,* (trans., N. M. Shaikh), Karachi: International Islamic Pub., 1981.

Bailey, V. and Wise, E., *Muhammad: his times and influence,* Edinburgh: W & R Chambers Ltd, 1976.

Bakhash, S., *The Reign of the Ayatollahs: Iran and the Islamic Revolution,* New York: Basic Books, 1984.

Cavendish, R., *The Great Religions,* London: Contact Pub., 1980.

Chapman, C., *Cross & Crescent,* England: Inter Varsity Press, 1995.

Chittick, W. C., *Sufism,* USA: Oneworld Pub., 2000.

Cragg, K., *The Call of the Minaret,* New York: Oxford University press, 1956.

Crittenden, P. W., *Islam,* London: Macmillan Education Ltd, 1972.

300

Dashti, A., *Twenty Three Years*, London: George Allen & Unwin, 1985.

Dennett, B., *Sharing God's Love with Muslims*, Sth. Holland: The Bible League, 1992.

El Droubie, Riadh, *Islam*, London: Ward Lock Educational Co., Ltd, 1983.

Geisler, N.L. & Saleeh, A., *Answering Islam*, USA: Baker Books, 1997.

Gilchrist, J., *The Textual History of the Qur'an and the Bible*, Reprinted by WEC International, 1987.

Gilchrist, J., *The Title of Jesus in the Qur'an and the Bible*, England: Roodepoort Mission Press, 1986.

Ginzberg, L. A., *A Commentary on the Palestinian Talmud*, New York, Vol. I, 1941.

Glubb, J. B., *A Short History of the Arab People*, London: Quartet Books, 1969.

Goldsmith, M., *Islam and Christian Witness*, London: Hodder and Stoughton, 1982.

Guillaume, A., *Islam*, London: Penguin Books, 1954.

Hahn, E., *Understanding Some Muslim Misunderstanding*, Ontario: The Fellowship of Faith (no date of print).

Haykal, M. H., *The Life of Muhammad*, Indianapolis: North American Trust Publications, 1976.

Heydt, H. J., *A Comparison of World Religions*, Pennsylvania: Christian Literature Crusade, 1976.

Hinnells, J. R., *Dictionary of Religions*, Great Britain: Penguin Books, 1984.

Hinnells, J. R., *Zoroastrianism and the Parsis*, Great Britain: Ward Lock Educational, 1981.

Ibn-Ghaisse, Salim, *Asrar Aal Muhammad (The Misteries of Muhammad's Descendants)*, Iran-Ghom: Translated by B. Alef, 1980? (1400 Hijri-Ghamari).

Ibn Hisham, *Sirat Rasul Allah, (The Life of Muhammad*, translation by R. E. Ibn M. Hamadani), Tehran: Ershad Islami Pub., 1998 (1377 Hijra).

Jadeed, I., *Did God Appear in the Flesh?*, Switzerland: The Good Way Rickon (no date of print).

Kamel, H., *Communicating the Gospel to Muslims*, USA: A.C.C. Pub., 1994.

Katsh, A. I., *Judaism and the Koran*, New York: A. S. Barnes and Company, Inc., 1962.

Khamaneie, A., *Ajubatol-esteftaat* (in Dari Farsi), Tehran: Saghalain Pub., 1997 (1376 Hijra).

R. Khomeini, *Tahrirolvasyleh*, Iran/Ghom: Darol Elm, 1990.

Khomeini, R., *Tozih Almasael*, Iran-Mashhad: Baresh Pub., 2000 (1379 Hijra).

Lang, D. M. (Editor), *Guide to Eastern Literature*, Great Britain: C. Tinling & Co. Ltd., 1971.

Langley, M., *Religions*, London: Lion Pub., 1981.

Machatschke, R., *Islam: The Basics*, London: SCM Press Ltd, 1995.

Mackey, S., *Passion and Politics*, USA: A Dutton Book Pub., 1992.

McCurry, D., *Now You Can Learn What Muslims Believe*, printed in USA (no date of print).

Mueller, M., ed., *Secret Books of the East,* Oxford: Krishna Press, 1897-1910.

Muhsin Khan, M., *Sahih Bukhari Vol.6, Hadith 71,* Published by Islamic University, Al Medina Al Munauwara, ND.

Nehls, G., *Christians Ask Muslims,* Nairobi: Life Challenge Pub., 1992.

Nicholson. R. A., *Literary History of the Arabs,* England: Curzon Press Ltd, 1993 (first published in 1907).

North Africa Mission, *Reaching Muslims Today,* India, 1988.

Otis, G., JR., *The Last of the Giants,* USA: Chosen Books, 1993.

Parrinder, G., *Jesus in the Qur'an,* Faber and Faber, 1965.

Parrinder, E. G., *A Book of World Religions,* Great Britain: Hulton Educational Pub., 1974.

Parshall, P., *New Paths in Muslim Evangelism,* USA: Baker Book House Company, 1992.

Parshall, P, *Beyond the Mosque,* USA:    Baker Book House Company, 1985.

Parshall, P, *The Cross and the Crescent,* USA: Tyndale House Pub. Inc., 1989.

Parshall, P *Inside the Community,* USA: Baker Books, 1994.

Rawlings, M., *Life-Wish: Reincarnation: Reality or Hoax,* Nashville: Thomas Nelson Inc., 1981.

Quilici, F., *Children of Allah,* USA: Chartwell Books Inc., 1978.

Sahih Al-Musim, *Hadith*

Savage, K., *The History of World Religions,* London: The Bodley Head, 1970.

Shahrestani, A. M. A., *Tozih-almelal (Almelal Valnahl)*, Iran: Translated by S. M. Jalali-Naieni, Eghbal Pub., 1982 (1361 Hijra).

Shephard, W. E., *Muslims Attitudes toward Judaism and Christianity,*

Sherratt, B. W. and Hawkin, D. J., *Gods and Men,* London: Blackie and Son Ltd, 1972.

Smith, R. B., *Mohammed and Mohammedanism,* London, 1889.

Tabari, Muhammad-bin Jarir, *Commentary on the Qur'an* (translated from Arabic into Persian 972-987 AD), Tehran: Tehran University Pub., 1977 (1356 Hijra).

Tabari, Muhammad-bin Jarir, *Tarikh-al-rosol val-molouk (The History of Prophets and Kings),* Tehran: translated from Arabic into Persian by Abolghasem Payandeh, Asatir Pub., 1996 (1375 Hijra).

Tames, R., *The Muslim World,* London: Macdonald & Co., Ltd., Pub., 1982.

Taylor, J. B., *Thinking about ISLAM,* Great Britain: Lutterworth Educational, 1971.

Thomas, H., *An Unfinished History of the World,* London: Hamish Hamilton, 1979.

Torrey, Ch. C., *The Jewish Foundation of Islam,* New York: 1933.

Watt, W. M., *Muhammad at Medina,* Oxford: Clarendon Press, 1956.

Whiting, R., *Religions of Man,* Great Britain: Stanley Thornes Pub., 1986.

Wiet, G., Elisseeff, V., Wolff P., and Naudou, J., *The Great Medieval Civilisations*(Vol. III), London: George Allen and Unwin Ltd., 1975.

Williams, J. A., *Islam,* Washington: Square Press, 1963.

304

Zacharias, R., *Jesus Among Other Gods,* USA: Word Publishing, 2000.

THE KORAN, translated by J. M. Rodwell, London: Everyman, 1994.

Other Editions for Comparisons:
The Qur'an, Text, Translation and Commentary by T. B. Irving, Tehran: Suhrawardi Research & Publication Center, 1998.

Alghoran-el-karim, translated into Persian by M. Elahi Ghomsheie, Iran: 1368 (Hijra).

KUR'N-I KERIM, translated under the chairmanship of A. Ozek, Madina: 1987.

The Avesta:
- Avesta: (Yasna, Gatha, Yashts, Visperd, Khordeh Avesta), research and translation into Persian by Hashem Razi, Forouhar Pub., 1995 (1374 Hijra).
- The Yasna; book 1 & 2, compilation and commentary in Persian by Pourdavood.
- Gathas (hyms), by Pourdavood, 1975 (1354) third edition.
- The Vendidad (books2, 3 and 4) translation in Persian by Hashem Razi, 1997 (1376).
- Visperd, reported by Pourdavood, second edition.
- Khordeh Avesta, edited by Rashid Shahmardan, Bombay-India: Published by P. P. Bharucha, Hon. Secy, The Iranian Zoroastrian Anjuman, 1929 (1308).

The Holy Bible, New International Version, USA: Zondervan Publishing House, 1989.

The International Standard Bible Encyclopedia, USA: W. B. Eerdmans Pub., 1988.

The World Book Encyclopedia, USA: 1983.

The New Bible Dictionary, London: Iter-Varsity, 1962.